Bredon Hill

Bredon Hill
A Guide to its Archaeology, History, Folklore & Villages

by

Brian Hoggard

Logaston Press

LOGASTON PRESS
Little Logaston Woonton Almeley
Herefordshire HR3 6QH
logastonpress.co.uk

First published by the author 1998
Published by Logaston Press 1999
2nd Revised edition published by Logaston Press 1999
Reprinted 2000, 2001
3rd Revised edition published by Logaston Press 2005
4th Revised edition published by Logaston Press 2009
Reprinted 2013

ISBN 978 1906663 18 6

Typeset by Logaston Press
and printed in Malta by
Gutenberg Press

Cover illustrations
Front: Parsons Folly and Kemerton Camp
Rear: Bambury Stone, Beckford Church,
cottage being re-thatched in Elmley Castle

Contents

Acknowledgements

For the arty photographs on page 6, thanks are due to Andy Tyler, BA, MA, freelance artist and illustrator who is available for commissions at 7 Camp Hill Avenue, Worcester. His other artwork can be viewed at www.andytyler.co.uk

Thanks are due to Worcestershire's County Archaeological Services and their Sites and Monuments Record, held at Woodbury Hall, University College Worcester, Henwick Grove, Worcester WR2 6AJ. The numbers listed in the references correspond with files they hold. Viewing is by appointment only.

The work of many authors and individuals have been used in creating this book. It would be difficult in this limited space to thank each one individually and it is hoped that the references provide sufficient acknowledgement for their efforts. The one important exception to this should be the Rev. R.H. Lloyd, whose *Bredon Hill and its Villages* was my first experience of local history. Without his interesting and informative book, this one may never have appeared. I hope that his book continues to sell in the same steady way that it has done since it was first published in 1967.

It is hoped that readers will consult and use the list of references to conduct their own further research into areas of the hill that they may feel I have neglected. If anyone with further information about the archaeology and folklore of the hill wishes to contact me, please write and send your information to me care of Logaston Press.

Introduction

A glance at an atlas shows that Bredon Hill is one of the only places for miles around that is not criss-crossed by roads. It is an isolated island of countryside which is not well enough known to have suffered the traumas that similar beauty spots have endured through mass tourism. Its summit rises to just under 1,000 ft, some 850 feet above the ring of villages that lie about its lower slopes. It is dotted with standing stones and Bronze Age barrows, has three Iron Age hill forts, a Norman castle, a holy well, a disappeared cave, and a folly — whilst a host of tales and folklore add further mystery. Indeed, Bredon Hill has long exerted a strange magnetism on the inhabitants of the villages that encircle it. Poets and novelists such as A.E. Housman, John Moore and Fred Archer have written about it.

Its name subtly recurs in several contexts which are a little less conventional than the poetry of Housman and the stories of Moore or Archer. Doreen Valiente in her *ABC of Witchcraft Past and Present* cites Bredon Hill as a place with witchcraft associations and notes a 'triangular alignment' of such sites with Meon Hill (Warwickshire) and a place called Seven Wells. Rosemary Ellen Guiley in *An Encyclopedia of Witches and Witchcraft* mentions the Bambury Stone as a place where witches gather around strange forces. The witchcraft associations more than likely have originated in garbled accounts of stories written by Fred Archer, which have included tales of witches on the hill. Harold Wilkins mentions the mysterious murder of Harry Dean at 'Death Quarry' on the hill in his work, *Mysteries: Solved and Unsolved*. Harry Dean was found dead in a quarry with his tie constricted about his neck — Wilkins blames this on an 'unseen entity' that strangled him in this 'open air temple of paranoiac fertility rites' (an abandoned quarry). Janet and Colin Bord say there is a legend that treasure is buried beneath the Bambury Stone in their *Atlas of Magical Britain*, though this is not a legend that I've otherwise come across.[1]

Whether all these legends and occult references to Bredon Hill are true or not, they certainly all attest to one thing. Bredon Hill has a mysterious feel to those who walk its slopes with an open mind. The feeling recalls the descriptions of our ancient pagan ancestors who had a deep reverence for boundaries, or liminal points in the landscape. Caves and springs, where contact with unseen underground forces was deemed possible, hill summits and dark forests, where supernatural forces were somehow closer — Bredon Hill has all of these (the cave is now lost, however).

There are sites that were of relevance to our pagan ancestors in the shape of the Bambury Stone, the King and Queen Stones and the stones at Bredon's Norton. Iron Age forts dating from around 200 BC or earlier exist at Conderton, Elmley and the summit itself. There are the remains of a Norman castle at Elmley Castle and lost chapels at St. Katherine's and Netherton. There are abandoned overgrown quarries, hidden natural pools, ancient oaks and an underground reservoir; even a few ghosts and a dead pirate — actually, more of a smuggler. This was Captain Bell who was responsible for one of the more unusual buildings on the slopes of Bredon Hill, at Kemerton. Ann Moore, in her *Curiosities of Worcestershire*, explains that he decided he wanted to build a kind of castle with his criminally obtained wealth, so in 1820 he transformed a row of labourers' cottages into what is now a very fancy large house with battlements and turrets. The house, known as Bell's Castle, is now a private residence. It is said that Captain Bell's more illegal activities were brought to the attention of the law and he was hanged in 1841. An illegitimate daughter from Cheltenham arranged for him to be buried at nearby Pershore Abbey — nowhere is his grave to be seen, however.[2]

Another unusual feature about the Hill is that, in addition to the usual wildlife (including badgers, foxes and deer), there is a slightly more frightening local resident, the 'Beast of Bredon'. Described as a large black cat, this animal has been sighted by many local people, mostly at the eastern end of the hill. The story about this beast first broke on the 21st April 1995 when a Mr Watkins of Ashton-under-Hill found some large paw prints in the mud near his home. This claim was accompanied by both photographs of the prints and supporting testimony of one Mr Figgett from Tewkesbury. He said that he saw the animal going through a hedge near the Westmancote turning between Bredon and Kemerton. Sightings elsewhere included that of the 24th April when the *Gloucestershire Echo* reported another sighting in Cirencester. By May 1995 reports of big cats in Gloucestershire and surrounding areas had reached the point where the Ministry of Agriculture had drafted in a tracker hound to try to locate one of the animals. Sightings of the black beast have far from diminished in the last four years. Many serious attempts have been made across Britain to catch one of these animals, mostly in the south-west of England, but none have proved successful as yet. The Beast of Bredon has had a serious effect on some locals. A Worcester lady I spoke to recently says that ever since she saw the 'beast' on Bredon Hill she has been concerned when out walking. This big cat is one of Bredon's more modern and tangible mysteries.[3]

Bredon Hill remains a mysterious place in many other ways and people still report strange experiences and 'atmospheres' when they've been out walking. The evidence of history, archaeology and folklore seems to attest to the fact that our pagan ancestors also had this feeling. The King and Queen Stones, the lost henge monument at Nafford, the holy well beneath the summit, and the highly significant alignment between the summit and British Camp on the Malvern Hills (see pp.15-16) all testify to the feeling that this place has been 'special' throughout history. Many other places possess this feeling, but within Worcestershire at least, Bredon Hill seems to have been the most important.

Brian Hoggard,
May 1999

General and Site Location Map

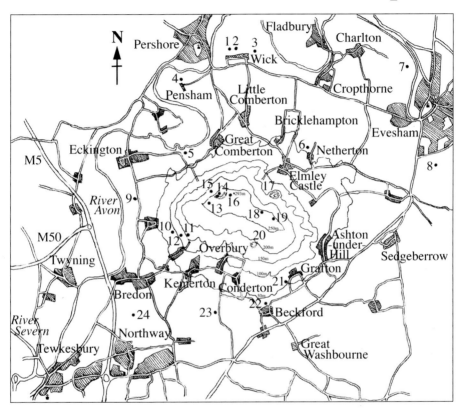

This list of sites includes those mentioned in the text, together with those ascertained from aerial photographs or documentary sources. Any dating or other information about these sites is as a result of archaeological excavation, comparison with other similar sites, field walking or stray finds. Should any readers want to conduct further research, the Sites and Monuments Record numbers are also included — their address is given in the Acknowledgements — followed by the grid reference in brackets. Sites marked with an [X] are not mentioned in the main text because there is nothing to see at the site. Many of these sites are Scheduled Ancient Monuments and so are protected by law. Please remember, do not stray from public rights of way without the prior permission of the landowner and follow the Countryside Code.

1. Aerial photography has revealed a 'ring-ditch', probably a 'ploughed-out' Bronze Age round barrow. SMR no 04539 (9616 4563). [X]

2. As per site 1 above, aerial photography has revealed another 'ploughed-out' ring-ditch. SMR no.04552 (9668 4569). [X]

3. The site of a cursus monument, again revealed through aerial photography at Wick. These are large rectilinear ditched enclosures with a presumed ritual function dating from the Neolithic (4500-2300BC). Such monuments are older than the circular or elliptical earthen henge monuments made famous by those containing stone circles like Stonehenge and Avebury. SMR no.05585 (975 453). [X]

4. These two ring-ditches revealed through aerial photography at Pensham are probably 'ploughed-out' Bronze Age burials. SMR nos.01269 (9422 4444) and 10060 (9435 4465). [X]

5. A fascinating group revealed through aerial photography within the parish of Eckington at Nafford. It appears to consist of two ring-ditches and a large henge monument probably dating from the Bronze Age, (2300-500BC). SMR nos.06061 (Henge) (9433 4176), 04064 (9439 4174) and 01265 (9400 4160). [X]

6. Another cursus monument revealed at Netherton near Elmley Castle by aerial photography. These large rectilinear ditched enclosures are thought to have been used for ritual purposes during the Neolithic (4500-2300BC). At this site there is also a pit alignment (function unclear) and another ring-ditch, presumably a 'ploughed-out' Bronze Age burial mound. SMR no.05564 (991 421). [X]

7. This ring-ditch (ploughed-out Bronze Age burial mound) was discovered through aerial photography. SMR no.10121 (0294 4502). [X]

8. A group of features revealed through aerial photography south of Evesham, comprising enclosures and more ring-ditches (presumably

Bronze Age burial mounds). SMR nos.06107 (0445 4140), 06108 (0445 4140), 04024 (0309 4087) and 10126 (0316 4111). [X]

9. It is unclear what type of feature these cropmarks near Bredon's Norton indicate, again revealed through aerial photography. SMR no.07648 (927 398). [X]

10. An impressive group of stones possibly being the remains of a megalithic tomb or a stone circle. See Bredon's Norton Stones pp.18-20. SMR no.07561 (9397 3872).

11. The King and Queen Stones. See pp.7-11 for details of these and the nearby round barrow. SMR no.04873 (9440 3860).

12. An impressive group of stones recently identified by the author exist at this site. It is not yet clear what they are but they may be the remains of another ancient monument (9435 3845). See Bredon's Norton Stones pp.18-20.

13. The site of a twin beaker burial which has been excavated. See p.21. SMR no.07324 (953 398). [X]

14. A group of prominent sites including Kemerton Camp, the Bambury Stone, Parsons' Folly, a cairn (now gone) and a cave (gone). There is lots to see here — refer to main text (958 402).

15. St Katherine's Well. SMR no.07686 (955 403). See pp.31-3.

16. It is recorded in the Sites and Monuments Record that a tumulus, probably a round barrow, once existed at this site. SMR no.10657 (9624 4027). [X]

17. Elmley Castle and Iron Age hill fort. See pp.26-9. SMR no.07263 (9795 4025).

18. A.C. Smith, in his folders at St. Helen's Record Office in Worcester, says that there used to be a cairn on the escarpment here. In his section on trackways he says, 'Near the Long Plantation above Elmley Park, where

one trackway crosses another, there once stood a Cairn, an old print of which is still in existence I believe. The place where it stood is known to this day as Monument Hill.' *Five folders compiled in 1932* by A.C. Smith, BA3624, Record Office, Fish Street, Worcester (973 396). [X]

19. A long mound at this site which could be a Neolithic (4500-2300BC) long barrow. It is large, being described as 10 by 4 metres, height 2 metres, higher at western end. SMR no.05008 (9788 3930).

20. Conderton Camp Iron Age hill fort. See pp.23-4, 26. SMR no.02907 (9714 3834).

21. Mr Wayne Perkins first drew my attention to this site. It appears to be a large upright standing stone standing just off the westernmost road to Grafton. It is hidden amongst vegetation but is well worth finding. See photograph p.12 (9843 3681).

22. Beckford Iron Age occupation site, revealed through aerial photography. This place was thoroughly excavated and the findings were published in Oswald, Adrian, 'Excavations at Beckford', *Transactions of the Worcestershire Archaeological Society*, 3rd series, vol 3, 1970-72, pp.7-53. SMR no.02908 (9762 3610). [X]

23. A group of ring-ditches and enclosures were revealed through aerial photography south of Kemerton. Excavations took place here and were published in Dinn, James and Evans, Jane, 'Aston Mill Farm, Kemerton: Excavations of a Ring-ditch, Middle Iron Age Enclosures, and a Grubenhaus', *Transactions of the Worcestershire Archaeological Society*, 3rd series, vol 12, 1990, pp5-66. This site was also featured in the 'Time-Team' programme in March 1999. SMR nos.10059 (9595 3585), 10277 (9520 3547), 10278 (9515 3587), 10279 (9549 3563) and 10280 (9550 3557). [X]

24. Another ring-ditch (probable ploughed-out Bronze Age burial mound) revealed through aerial photography. SMR no.06585 (9250 3570). [X]

Geology & Geomorphology

Bredon Hill is the largest of the Cotswold outliers and is the only Cotswold hill to lie fully within Worcestershire, though part of the escarpment at Broadway, including Broadway Tower, is also within the county. They are, incidentally, two of the highest points on this range of hills and both sport rather distinctive 18th century follies — making it easy to identify Worcestershire's Cotswold territories.

Geologically speaking, the easiest way to view Bredon Hill is as an upside-down cake. It is capped by oolitic limestone from the Jurassic geological period. This limestone is a sedimentary rock which consists of millions of small fossilised sea creatures and other particles which have been cemented together. This was once a sea floor but subsequent changes in the earth's crust have forced the Cotswold region upwards. This 'oolite' limestone is often known as roestone because it looks like fish eggs when viewed very closely.[1]

The limestone cap creates the characteristic steep escarpment that follows the north and west faces of the majority of the Cotswold hills. Beneath this limestone cap are layers of softer clay-rock, known broadly as the lias layers. This creates a kind of aquifer, where the water contained by the limestone cannot permeate downwards through less porous clay. As a result the water is forced outwards beneath the limestone to form a spring line.[2] St. Katherine's Well at the foot of the steep escarpment below the summit is a good example of this, from which flows a picturesque stream. There are many other springs around the hill, but several are now managed and have lost much of their natural appeal. Another geological layer, between the upper and lower lias, consists of marlstone. This rock is harder than lias clays

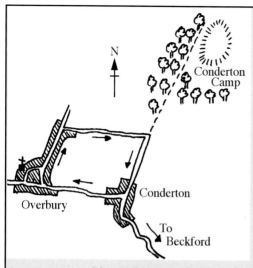

Conderton & Overbury walk

This is a gentle circular walk which will take up to an hour at a leisurely pace.

Find your way to the village of Conderton and locate the Yew Tree pub at its centre. Park somewhere safely up the lane next to the pub — and if you don't fancy a drink just yet, then you can begin your walk.

Starting from the pub, turn right onto the main village road towards Overbury. As you progress on this walk you will have the opportunity to admire many attractive Cotswold stone buildings on this gentle, southern side of the hill. Approaching the edge of the village you will have the opportunity to pop in to the Bredon Hill Pottery which has its workshops and showroom here. Continue on the main road towards Overbury once you've finished at the Pottery.

Overbury village centre is highly attractive and has all the key components of a picturesque English village — a shop, cricket ground, church and manor. Before you explore the fine Norman church and surrounding buildings, make a note of the road leading up the hill to the right as you'll need to walk it to complete the walk.

This main road up the hill from the village centre gets gradually steeper as you progress along it, but the high status dwellings from different periods that adorn either side of this road will engage your attention so much that you will hardly notice the ascent.

At the first junction you will have to follow the road leading to the right. If you are feeling puffed you can take a rest here on a strategically placed bench. At first this road is quite steep, so take it slowly. As it levels out and the buildings become fewer a wonderful view across to the main Cotswold range will open before you. Continue along this road until it drops steeply down again and turns to the right, heading back towards Conderton village. The lane follows a stream and will lead you back to your vehicle and the pub.

and is what has created the spurs around the hill which form steep little valleys, the marlstone being more resistant to weathering.[3]

Bredon Hill is particularly prone to landslips and slope failures of other kinds. This recurring natural hazard began towards the end of the last Ice Age, about 18,000 years ago and persists to this day.[4] The last Ice Age in Britain is known as the Devensian — during this period Bredon Hill was just outside the limits of the main ice sheet which covered most of the north of the British Isles. At its maximum extent the ice sheet lay only 35 miles to the north[5] and the hill was subject to the very cold conditions experienced at the edge of an ice sheet, known as the periglacial environment.[6] Towards the end of this period the lias clays below the limestone cap of the hill swelled and contracted with extreme fluctuations of moisture and temperature. This caused warping and cracking in the limestone cap along natural faults, leaving gaps known as 'gulls' between the major blocks in the bedrock.[7] The increased slope angle caused by these processes in the limestone cap, where large blocks are forced to 'lean', means that the caprock moved down the sides of the hill — a process known as cambering. This material, including soil, collects at the foot of the slope and becomes mixed with water from the spring line, in a kind of 'mixing bowl' area. When the 'bowl' builds up to a certain pressure, it causes the material to slip down the hillside.[8] These landslips can be dramatic and remove large areas of the hill — for example Kemerton Camp's northern and western defences were probably removed through the 'cambering' of the limestone layer. The area of the hill known as Woollashill, which is beneath the limestone layer, has been subject to large landslips in recent times and is the focus of much academic attention. It was thought that the big landslips always occurred following prolonged periods of rain, but it has now been shown that whether the 'bowl' is full or not is also a crucial factor.[9] It is likely that the landscape is more stable now than it was in past times, because many water sources have now been channelled for agricultural purposes.

Even so, the ground is still moving on Bredon Hill. In the large field between Upper Westmancote and Bredon's Norton Stones an area of woodland has been removed in the past 25 years. Where previously the roots of the trees maintained the hill slope stability, the ground is now slipping, showing many breaks in the turf. It is possible that this might lead to a major slip at some point. The Woollashill site is still active too. Recent research by Vicky Mowbray of University College Worcester has demonstrated the continuing transformation of the landscape at this site between 1997 and 1998.[10]

The veneration of natural exposures of rock is of relevance to Bredon Hill and is a key theme in this book. The Bambury Stone and the King and Queen Stones, which are large natural outcrops of 'gull rock' — fragments of rock which have become cemented together inside cracks in the bedrock by calcium-rich water[11] — have apparently been regarded as sacred for an extremely long time. The same veneration of natural stones occurs in Hertfordshire where a similar type of stone conglomerate known as 'pudding-stone' exists. These formed where pebbles were cemented together by silicate, and tend to occur in much more portable sizes (ranging from 10cm to 2m across) than the 'gull rock' of Bredon Hill, but have played a major role in Hertfordshire folklore. They were used as charms against witchcraft in more recent periods and pieces of it have been used as foundation stones for churches.[12] In very recent times some Hertfordshire researchers have been looking at the larger examples of these stones with regard to the study of linear alignments such as that described in the Folklore section between Pershore Abbey and Bredon Hill summit. Generally, little attention has been given to the study of naturally occurring landforms having a special cultural or spiritual significance in archaeological literature. In the case of Bredon Hill however, and possibly in some areas of Hertfordshire, the veneration of geology appears to be integral to understanding the sacred landscape of our ancestors.

Standing Stones & the Early Presence of Man

Bredon Hill is notable for its standing stones, the best known of which are the King and Queen Stones and the Bambury Stone, though there are others. The King and Queen Stones and the Bambury Stone are not typical standing stones. Standing stones are usually naturally shaped or rough-hewn pieces of rock which have been placed pointing upwards either singly, in rows or in circles in their chosen location most probably during the Bronze Age (2300 - 800BC). Gloucestershire and Herefordshire have many standing stones though few stone circles; Worcestershire has none of the latter — unless Bredon's Norton Stones are eventually proved to have been a stone circle at some time.

Theories for the symbolism and function of standing stones are many and varied and range from simple territorial markers to being part of a complex ritual symbolising a spirituality and knowledge of the night sky. Single standing stones have been described as, '... at once the simplest and most enigmatic of megaliths.'[1] Often there is a significant lunar alignment related to these stones, or else they may figure in alignments with other sites of the same date. Some stones are known to possess a magnetic quality which will affect a compass needle — but whether such magnetism was known to the people who erected them or not is the subject of some debate. Much folklore connected to 'fairy lights' and other strange forces often occurs in connection with standing stones. Paul Devereux in his book *Places of Power*[2] has attempted to measure naturally occurring energies at sites such as these to see if there may be some natural anomalies which may be responsible for inducing altered states — he has provided some interesting theories which appear to be very reasonable.

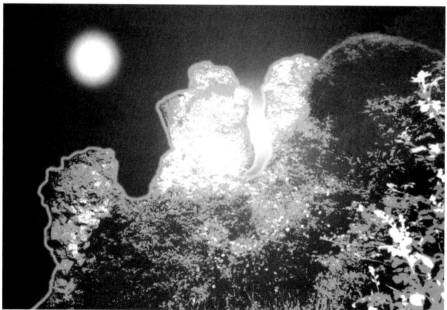

Top: The Bambury, or Elephant, Stone
Bottom: The King and Queen Stones

6

Shaped or rough-hewn standing stones appear to have been objects of considerable significance to our ancestors. However, the King and Queen Stones and the Bambury Stone are naturally occurring, for they are formed of 'gull' rock. 'Gull' rock is so named as it has been formed in cracks or 'gulls' in the bedrock, and has been described by Les Morris, a local geomorphologist, as '... a tough limestone made out of brecciated oolite rubble which has been cemented by calcareous tufa.'[3] Simply put this means that fragments of rock were weathered or broken off and fell into a crack in the rock where they were then cemented together by calcium rich water. The shape of the crack would have determined the shape of the resultant stone which would have been left as a 'standing stone' either once the surrounding rock had been quarried away, the 'gull' rock being unsuitable as a building stone, or once the surrounding material had slid away in a landslip.

Both the Bambury Stone and the King and Queen Stones have healing folklore attached to them and, as stated in the introduction, are considered 'places of power' by modern witches. Much of the folklore and belief which surrounds megaliths may be a continuation of much earlier practices, or may just dimly reflect an awe and belief about such stones held by our ancestors who were acutely aware of their environment and landscape. In the absence of pollution, noise and electronic diversions, subtle natural forces may have had a far greater perceived effect on the mind than is currently considered normal. Reinforced by belief the effects must have been considerable — certainly enough to expend enormous effort in creating standing stones and positioning them in perceived 'sacred' places with significant alignments to the moon, hills or other markers on the horizon.

The King and Queen Stones are in fact three stones, and are situated in a line on a steep south-west facing bank, the shortest stone being highest up the hill and the tallest at the bottom of the line. If they have been left standing after a landslip, then their tops may represent the old ground level.[4]

The obvious question is why are three stones named 'The King and Queen Stones'? The antiquarian Edwin Lees, while addressing members of the Worcestershire Naturalists' Club at the site in 1873, speculated that the upper two stones might once have been joined, as their tops nearly touch. He added that the practice of passing sick people through the holes in stones to heal them may once have been practised here. The

The King and Queen Stones

'passing through' ritual is one that has been observed throughout the world but the most famous British example is at Men-an-Tol near Madron in Cornwall where two standing stones have a circular sculpted 'wheel' of rock between them through which people crawl in order to obtain healing. The local historian, Reverend Lloyd also intimated that this practice may have occurred at this site, whilst the local authoress Mrs Jerome Mercier of Kemerton also seems to have thought that the stones were once joined. She wrote a children's story, *By the King and Queen*, published in 1906, which contains a cartoon of some 'Druids' standing next to what is allegedly the King and Queen Stones. They are portrayed as two stones, one of them having a hole. This theory seems convincing and certainly explains the naming of the stones. As for the origin of the 'passing through' practice, it may be that a holed stone was seen to crudely represent the female figure, while the single standing stone represented the male. About 20 feet south of the stones there is another single standing stone that appears to be made of harder rock. There is no explanation for its presence other than it being a freak geological feature.[5]

A little further south of the King and Queen Stones there is a round barrow with some more stones next to it. This barrow was recorded by the

8

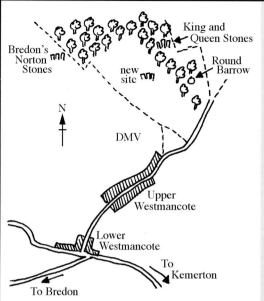

King and Queen Stones

Bredon's Norton Stones

new site

Round Barrow

N

DMV

Upper Westmancote

Lower Westmancote

To Kemerton

To Bredon

Exploring sites on the south-western corner of Bredon Hill

Park to the north of Upper Westmancote where the narrow road becomes a dirt track.

For the King and Queen Stones follow the dirt track up the hill until you reach a fork where you take the track to your left. Across a field to your left on private land there is a clump of tall trees which surmount the round barrow. Continue up the track until it turns sharply left and then immediately right again. After 10m or so the King and Queen Stones should be visible in the undergrowth at the edge of the wood on your left. This is a short but steep walk taking up to half an hour to reach the stones. The summit can be reached from here if you follow the waymarked track and then keep to the right through fields. At the end of these you turn right into a wood — travel through the wood and then follow the path to the left which will take you to the summit. This is a beautiful walk taking in total up to two hours to reach the summit if taken at a leisurely pace.

For Bredon's Norton Stones travel down the road from where you park until you reach a sharp left bend, where there's a farm gate to your right. Go over the style and follow the muddy track round through the field until you reach two farm gates which appear before you. Take the right hand gate and follow the hedge along the left hand side of the long field. The fields to your left on the other side of the hedge contain the subtle earthworks of a deserted medieval village. About half way along the field you will notice the unstable landscape to the right where the wood has been removed. At the top of this area is the new stone site referred to in the text — please keep to the rights of way however. At the end of the field you cross a stile into the next field in which you keep to the right. Bredon's Norton Stones will appear before you.

Woolhope Naturalists' Field Club and also by the Reverend Lloyd.[6] Most round barrows were built in Britain during the Bronze Age, though some were constructed during the Iron Age (700BC to the Roman invasion in 43AD) and the Roman occupation (43AD to the fifth century AD). Even the Saxons built some round barrows. It is impossible to know from which period the barrow dates until a professional archaeological excavation is carried out at the site — although if other nearby monuments are taken into account, an educated guess would place it earlier than the Roman period, and probably in the Bronze Age.

The stones adjacent to the barrow are related to an activity that used to take place at the King and Queen Stones. Both Lloyd and Lees talk about the declaration of a Court Leet for the Oswaldslow Hundred which used to occur at these stones — a Hundred being the old administrative area (similar to a district) and a Court Leet the local law court (a Leet was a smaller administrative area, roughly equivalent to a large parish). To explain why a legal assembly was held high up on a hillside at an ancient site, Edwin Lees pointed out that 'the holding of these formal ceremonies at sites so ancient and venerable bestowed an authority as ancient and immovable as the rock itself.'[7] In this he infers that the Court Leet was held here because of the sanctity of the place. Another indication of the site's sacredness is that it used to be whitewashed prior to the holding of the court — a very similar ceremony existed at the Bawdstone on the Roaches in Derbyshire, which was whitewashed on the morning of May 1st as part of the Beltane celebrations.[8] Beltane was one of the eight old pagan festivals, along with Lughnasa, Imbolc and Samhain (Halloween), the festivals of Midsummer and Midwinter — the solstices, and the Spring and Autumn equinoxes, where the sun rises and sets due east and west.

At the Court Leet people were punished for their crimes and it is this which explains the presence of the stones at the barrow south of the King and Queen Stones — they are the remains of stocks.[9] It is likely that a whipping post and gibbet once existed here too. The situation of it next to a barrow is rather canny, as it inclines the poor criminal to dwell on mortality. This sense of mortality would have been heightened as locals knew that the part of Bredon Hill known as Woollashill took its name from Wolves' Hill, owing to the large number of these predators that abounded there at the time of the Norman Conquest.

*The round barrow near the King and Queen Stones,
with one of the stones that formed the stocks*

There are two other very different factors which may contribute to the sanctity of these stones. The first is that the position of a twin Beaker Burial dating from the Bronze Age in the field adjacent to Kemerton Camp at the hill's summit is such that the view is drawn to the south-west — the direction of the King and Queen Stones.[10] This may provide the earliest archaeological evidence supporting the sacredness of this site — apart from the round barrow just south of the stones. Other evidence for the sacredness of the King and Queen Stones comes from the close proximity of Bredon's Norton Stones and the newly identified site near these. These are referred to on pp.18-20. A more recent and slightly different piece of evidence should at least cause people to regard the site with some solemnity and respect when visiting — during the early summer of 1998 a tree was planted at the base of the lower of the three stones. On the tag attached to it was the explanation that the cremated remains of a man who had died on the 6th of May 1998 had been deposited at the site. This man obviously had a deep love or reverence for the site.

At the summit of the hill, within a depression next to Parsons' Folly, lie several large stones, again formed of 'gull' rock. The largest of these has a rather elephantine appearance and as a result is known locally as the 'elephant stone', though on maps it is marked as the Bambury Stone.[11] 'Gull' rock does not make very suitable building material and it is probable that these stones were left over from a small quarry at the site — the cause of the depression. There is no apparent physical indication of when this quarrying took place but the antiquarian Jabez Allies, writing in the 1840s, thought that the quarry was used to build the inner rampart of Kemerton Camp which surrounds the hilltop. This would mean that the quarrying took place around 100BC. In a 1985 article by Bruce Watson, however, there is a map that describes the depression as a post-medieval quarry pit, although on what evidence it is not clear.[12]

It is possible that there were once more 'gull' rocks in this area. Apart from loss through landslides, a common event on the hill, Les Morris notes that, 'Other impressive masses have been carted downhill and used

as ornamental rockery stones in the gardens of Woollashill [Woollas Hall]'.[13] Both the King and Queen Stones and the Bambury Stone consist of 'gull' rock and it is possible that other outcrops of it also existed. The large upright standing stone recently discovered at Grafton by Wayne Perkins may be another example of an ancient sacred 'gull' rock.

It seems, fortunately, that the stones that Allies recorded when he visited the summit remain on the hill. When he visited the Bambury Stone he made a clear record of what he found:

Wayne Perkins with the possible standing stone discovered at Grafton

The Bambury Stone in the foreground with Parsons' Folly on the skyline

It stands within about 40 yards of the South-West end of the inner trench. It is situated a little within the entrance of an oblong basin or amphitheatre, near the Western focus of the ellipse, and is about twenty yards in circumference ... at the distance of about six yards before it, Westward, nearer the precipice, there is another stone about eleven yards in circumference, and about sixteen yards further Westwards, at the precipice, is a third stone, about ten yards in circumference and two yards high. There is also another stone, behind and to the East of the Bambury stone, which measures about eight yards in circumference. All these stones are nearly in a line with each other and stand in an Easterly and Westerly direction.[14]

One of these stones, however, now appears to be lodged half way down the steep escarpment beneath the stones.

The Reverend Lloyd's claim in 1967 that the stones were once one large stone at the summit that fell and broke into pieces 'about a hundred years ago' seems to be inaccurate. Although landslips have often occurred on this hill, Jabez Allies noted that the stones stood in a straight east-west line 126 years before Lloyd wrote his account. Also, Dr Derham wrote in 1713 that there were '... one or more vast stones ...' at the summit.[15]

Allies' description of the east-west orientation of the stones leads one to appreciate the wider orientation of the landscape as a whole. In pagan Britain and many other parts of the world there were four major solar festivals. These occurred at the two solstices in mid-winter and mid-summer which mark our nearest and furthest positions from the sun, and at the two equinoxes which are the mid-points between the two solstices. These latter festivals are particularly interesting because the sun rises and sets exactly due east and west if the landform the sun is rising or setting behind is roughly the same latitude and altitude as the point of observation. Due west of the Bambury Stone the sun would set behind British Camp (alias Herefordshire Beacon) on the Malvern Hills at the equinoxes. Likewise, the sun would appear to rise behind Bredon Hill summit at the equinoxes when viewed from British Camp. It seems probable that whether or not the stones stood in the distant past as they are now, the inhabitants of these two forts would have been aware of this natural alignment at the equinoxes.[16] This may have served as a calendar which marked the change in the seasons and could have indicated to the inhabitants when to sow or harvest. The chain of the Malvern Hills would also have served as a rough north-south indicator allowing those who lived on Bredon a certain spatial awareness unobtainable at less well situated places. Before cities and street lights appeared in our islands it was normal for people to be aware of the phases of the moon, the positions of the planets and any unusual astronomical phenomenon, simply by stepping outside and looking at the sky.[17] One can assume that those who inhabited Bredon Hill's summit and British Camp were particularly well placed to be knowledgeable beyond the norm about such matters.

There is a piece of folklore which seems to suggest the importance of the Bambury Stone when viewed in conjunction with this equinoctial alignment. There is a tradition of a burial path connecting Bredon Hill to Brailes in Warwickshire. A burial path, in conventional understanding, is a right of way that is established by a funeral procession's choice of route. Therefore, if a procession chose to cross a farmer's field, that route would thereafter constitute a right of way. The problem with this particular burial path is that it is 23 miles long, not a particularly easy distance to cover when carrying a coffin. The first person to describe the path in any detail was Alfred Woodward in an appendix to Peter Drinkwater's 1979 *Soliloquies of Old Shipston*, but he was originally informed of it by reading J. Harvey Bloom's 1929 *Folklore, Old Customs and Superstitions in Shakespeare Land*.[18] To walk the path as he describes it would leave one very tired and slightly dizzy, for it meanders somewhat and appears to be a collection of shorter burial paths joined together. He cites no evidence to support his described route and one has to wonder about his accuracy. The 1981 *Haunted Warwickshire* by Meg Elizabeth Atkins is equally vague about the path, but seems to at least have hit upon one way of interpreting it. She surmises, after exploring how unlikely a 23 mile long burial path would be, that, '... the belief in a path linking Brailes Hill and the Iron Age fort at Bredon gives rise to the possibility that here oral transmission has perpetuated — inevitably in a distorted form — the existence of a ley.'[19] By this she means that it is possible that the original path was not a burial path but a sacred route of some kind — perhaps that it was a spirit road or some other ancient perceived sacred way the memory of which has become distorted over time.

The burial path's route between Bredon and Brailes does indeed seem to be a 'ley' of some kind. If the straight east-west equinox line between Bredon Hill summit and British Camp is extended eastwards, it eventually reaches Castle Hill at Brailes — seemingly verifying the ancient sacred route theory. Perhaps, then, this burial path is really a solar alignment route. Jabez Allies, who didn't mention the equinox alignment, thought that the name Bambury meant 'sacred to the sun'.[20] This becomes yet more interesting when it is noted that even further eastwards the line reaches the town of Banbury. *En route* the line passes through Hinton-on-the-Green crossroads, Saintbury Cross and Dover's Hill on the Cotswolds. Perhaps, as I called it in a 1996 article for *The Ley Hunter*, this really is a 'dead sunny' alignment.[21]

The tradition of going to kiss the Bambury Stone for good luck on Good Friday is one shared with many other stones around Britain.[22] Locally, however, the same tradition occurs at the Pekket Rock in Habberley Valley near Kidderminster. This beautiful valley has as its centrepiece the towering natural sandstone 'horn' of the Pekket which has steps worn into it on one

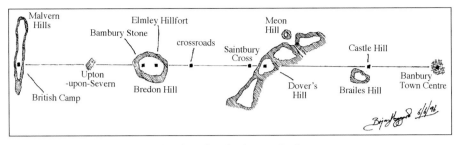

Map showing the 'dead sunny' alignment

side where people have ascended to the summit over the centuries. This tradition is probably the result of local Catholics attempting to continue their forms of Easter worship after the Reformation. Alternatively, it may be a relic of our ancient pagan past because Easter used to be a festival of the goddess Ostara, symbolised by a hare.[23] Not only has this festival been Christianized, but it is now represented by the rabbit, or 'bunny', a creature imported as a source of food soon after the Norman Conquest.

There is also a legend that the Bambury Stone will go for a drink from the River Avon when it hears the bells of Pershore Abbey strike midnight. Such a legend is often associated with ancient standing stones and so may be evidence in support of the antiquity of the stones, contradicting the notion that they are the remains of a post-medieval quarry. Another piece of folklore that possibly supports this is that the Bambury Stone is also reputed to have healing properties.[24]

The fact that there is an impressive solar alignment and 'burial path' that focuses on Bredon Hill summit where there are stones with a rich folklore, indicates both a sacred hilltop and stones that have been regarded as sacred for many centuries. In addition there used to be a cairn (see p.34), a sacred spring (see p.32-3) and a cave.

The cave is something of a mystery. In the eighteenth century it was not uncommon to find that those who wrote about and were interested in science and natural history were often clergymen. It is to one such clergyman, Dr Derham, a Fellow of the Royal Society, that we owe our thanks for apparently being the only person to have documented the existence of Bredon Hill's long since vanished cave. In 1713 he wrote *Physico-Theology, or a Demonstration of the Being and Attributes of God from his Works and Creation*, which was reprinted 11 times within the next 50 years. It was also translated into French, Swedish and German. Derham

16

thought (along with many contemporaries) that the creatures and natural landscape of the earth, '… bear Testimony to their infinite Workman; and that they exceed all humane Skill so far, as that the most exquisite Copies and Imitations of the best Artists, are no other than rude bungling Pieces to them.' The prevailing view in this period was that the magnificent works of nature were sufficient evidence in themselves for a deity.[25] Luckily for us, Dr Derham chose Bredon Hill as an example in his discussion on caves. The description is impressive, and while talking about caves containing stalactites (hanging down) and stalagmites (going up), he says:

> Such like caves as these I have myself met with in England; particularly on the very top of Bredon Hill in Worcestershire, near the precipice, facing Pershore, in or near the old fortress, called Bemsbury Camp, I saw some years ago such a cave, which, if I mis-remember not, was lined with those stalactical stones on the top and sides. On the top they hung like icicles, great and small, and many lay on the ground. They seemed manifestly to be made by an exudation or exstillation of some petrifying juices out of the rocky earth there. On the spot, I thought it might be from the rains soaking through, and carrying with it impregnations from the stone, the hill being there all rocky. Hard by the cave is one or more vast stones, which, if I mistake not, are incrusted with this sparry, stalactical substance, if not wholly made of it.[26]

The old fortress he refers to as Bemsbury Camp must be what is now called Kemerton Camp. There are two good clues to the exact whereabouts of the cave in his description — that the cave faces Pershore, and that 'Hard by the cave is one or more vast stones … which … are incrusted with this sparry, stalactical substance …'. This is presumably a reference that includes the Bambury Stone.

The event that destroyed the cave must have occurred between Derham's description of the cave in 1713 and the publication of Jabez Allies' book *The British, Roman and Saxon Antiquities and Folklore of Worcestershire* in the 1840s. Allies' book carefully describes the summit with a map showing the fort and the Bambury Stone, but with no indication of a cave. As landslips are rather common on this hill it is possible that this is what destroyed the cave. Alternatively, it is worthy of note that Parsons' Folly was built in the late eighteenth century very close to the possible location of the cave. It may be that the building of the folly destabilised the earth and caused the cave to collapse.

The existence of the cave transforms the vision of life on the summit. It could have served as a shelter for Stone and Bronze Age people before Kemerton Camp was constructed in the Iron Age. After the fort was built the cave could have served as a larder, keeping food cool and uncontaminated, though it is more likely that storage pits were used as at Conderton Camp.[27] The fact that the Holy Well of St. Katherine (see pp.31-3) and the Bambury Stone are so close to the cave possibly meant that it had more mystical than practical appeal. It may even have been regarded as a 'liminal' site, where the mysterious forces of the dark underworld were somehow closer. What a shame this cave has now gone.

Other standing stones, Bredon's Norton Stones, were mentioned earlier. These impressive stones stand alongside a path linking Upper Westmancote to the Manor at Bredon's Norton, beside Aldwick Wood. They are different to the King and Queen Stones and the Bambury Stone because they appear to have been moved to the site. The group consists of a cluster of boulders and one large, flat stone that has been worn, or rubbed smooth on one side. The Worcestershire Sites and Monuments Record records them as a suspected fallen long barrow which would mean that they date from the Neolithic period (4500-2300BC), the large stone being the suspected capstone from the tomb, and the boulders the old walls of the chamber(s).[28] Long barrows usually had a forecourt off which led a passage to the internal chamber(s) where ancestral remains might be kept. There is no evidence of the earth that once covered it or the passage that may have existed. Good examples of long barrows of this type dot the Cotswold escarpment in neighbouring Gloucestershire — such as Nympsfield, Uley and Belas Knap.

An alternative explanation for these stones was offered to me by Mrs Lily O'Sullivan from Westmancote in 1994. She recalls that when she lived in the area in the 1950s this area was all scrubland, much like some of the higher slopes on the hill and the stones were arranged in a circle with the large, smooth capstone in the centre. The reason for their current

Bredon's Norton Stones

grouping next to a boggy stream is that a local farmer 'cleared' the land for cultivation.[29] If this is true, then the stone circle would probably have been a late Neolithic or early Bronze Age monument possibly dating between 3500 and 1500BC.

There has not yet been a thorough archaeological examination of the site so the hypothesis that it was once a long barrow is based on comparison of the remains with long barrow sites elsewhere. Mrs O'Sullivan's suggestion that these may once have been a stone circle is equally plausible and probably more simple to investigate. The siting of the 'barrow' at the edge of the field in a boggy area is suggestive of the stones being moved and many locals will attest to the fact that farming has encroached upon the slopes of the hill since the Second World War.

An archaeological field visit to the site in the 1970s recorded another group of stones of similar size positioned only ten metres away to the southwest which have now disappeared — presumably through farming practice.[30] Very recently another very large stone has become exposed within five metres of the stones where a small shack has been demolished.

Yet another large group of stones has very recently been identified nearby.[31] In the long field between Aldwick Wood and Upper Westmancote there was once a piece of woodland which separated the field into two. Where this woodland has been cleared the land is beginning to slip — making the limits of the now vanished wood very obvious. At the top of this unstable landscape there is a large group of unworked stones that may be the remains of an ancient monument. Research into these stones is ongoing but if they are the remains of an ancient site then this area has probably the highest density of surviving ancient sacred monuments in Worcestershire. The Bredon's Norton Stones, this new site, the King and Queen Stones and the round barrow near to them are very closely grouped and may be evidence that there was an ancient settlement near here. This would confirm archaeologist Nicholas Thomas' hypothesis that the twin Beaker burial at the top of the hill was oriented to the south and south-west so as to be connected with a settlement on that side of the hill.[32] This is a significant sacred landscape and it should be treated with care.

The Bronze Age to Recent Times

Definite evidence for use and occupation of the hilltop begins in the Bronze Age (approx 2300 - 700 BC). A twin Beaker burial (burials which contain large earthenware vessels known as 'beakers') was excavated by Nicholas Thomas in Well Gate Field adjacent to Kemerton fort at the summit of the hill in the 1960s. He states that the barrow dominates the ground to the south and south-west (facing the King and Queen Stones) and surmised that the burial must have been connected with a settlement on that side of the hill. The burial is described as 'A low irregular mound of limestone rubble, about 32ft in diameter, [which] covered a rock-cut grave which contained the skeleton of a tall, sturdy middle-aged male, to which that of a young athletically built female had been subsequently added.' Two Bronze Age Bell Beakers were found along with some arrowheads, a flint scraper and a thick bone pin.[1]

A bronzeworks at the site also indicates settlement during this period. By 200BC, in the Iron Age, a small town became well established and was enclosed by the first defensive bank and ditch. Around 100BC a second, outer rampart was built, possibly as a result of new defensive ideas, or due to population increase or the arrival of outsiders. These two ramparts form what is known as the Iron Age hill fort of Kemerton Camp. The Iron Age is generally considered to begin around 700BC and end with the Roman conquest of England in 43AD. The fort which contains both the Bambury Stone and Parsons' Folly within its circuit, is 22 acres in extent and has two main defences which are in a comparatively good state of preservation. Excavations by Hencken between 1935 and 1937 have revealed some details of both the construction of the defences as well as some internal

The ramparts of Kemerton Camp

features.[2] At first glance it seems that the reason why there are no defences on the north and west sides is because of the very steep natural precipice which seems to do this job adequately. It is thought, however, that ditches once existed on these sides too, but were destroyed by landslips which have often struck the summit.[3] For example, one occurred in 1804 which took away several acres on the north-east edge of the hill.[4] The inner rampart contained evidence of having a timber frame or lacing and originally had 'a simple overlapping entrance at the south-east corner.' This was later superseded by a 30m long inturned and stone-lined entrance. The outer rampart was stone-faced and the north-west entrance had a very complex gateway construction. The inner entrance passageway proved to be the site of a massacre where the remains of about 50 mutilated individuals aged between 25 and 35 were discovered along with many weapons.[5] Inside the ramparts there has been found evidence of domestic huts, and pottery finds have been dated to between the fourth and first centuries BC.

This massacre seems very alien to the quite beautiful views that reward the walker on reaching the summit. The defensive potential that these views provide, however, was the reason for the hill fort being built here. In the time of the fort, the view west would have been dominated by the Malvern Hills with British Camp and Midsummer Hill forts being very obviously perched atop the ridge — the location of these two forts would have been made more apparent by the smoke from the fires within them. The floodplains of the rivers Severn and Avon would also have been major landmarks with large marshy areas extending either side of them and woodland beyond these. To the south and east the main Cotswold escarpment would have been wooded with occasional clearances containing yet more hill forts. The majority of the forts visible from Bredon Hill would have belonged to the tribal group known as the Dobunni who occupied (approximately) the region now comprising north Gloucestershire, Herefordshire, Worcestershire and the West Midlands. Tensions with the neighbouring tribes to the north and north-west (Cornovii), east (Catuvellauni), west (Silures) and south (Atrebates) may frequently have flared into trouble and there were also invasions from tribes on the continent.[6] As if this wasn't enough the Romans invaded in 43 AD. Further problems may have been encountered with wild bulls, boar, bears and wolves — wild ponies and beavers would, I assume, have posed slightly less of a hazard.[7]

It is considered that people lived here well into the first century AD, unlike the evidence of occupation from Conderton Camp, east of here.[8] This Iron Age hill fort on the south-eastern portion of the hill faces the nearest hills in the main Cotswold escarpment, and is one of a triangle of Iron Age forts on Bredon Hill constructed by the Dobunni tribe, the third being at Elmley Castle. Covering a mere 1.2 acres it is the smallest hill fort on the hill and is positioned on a low spur but, despite its relatively low altitude compared to Kemerton and Elmley forts, it holds a commanding view of the valley between Bredon Hill and the other Cotswolds. The three forts are thought to have been built at roughly the same time, which indicates not only a fairly large population, but also a strong group sense of the need to defend the territory.

The outline of Conderton Camp on the hillside across the gully

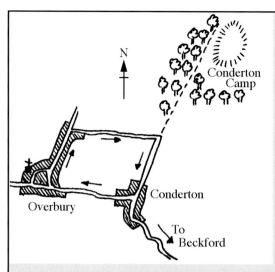

Exploring Conderton Camp

It is possible to leave your car in the village of Conderton, and then follow the track up the hill until you reach a very sharp left bend. You will see a track leading ahead of you. Follow the track until it takes a right turn, at this point you continue straight on into the fields always keeping to the right of way with the woods to your left. Conderton Camp sits atop the spur to your right. This is a gentle walk taking up to an hour to reach the Camp.

There is a strong spring near the foot of this fortified spur, ensuring a good water supply for its inhabitants. A highly unusual point about this fort is that it has a cross rampart with drystone facing separating it into two parts, one roughly double the other in size. The fort has entrances to the north and south, sited along the spine of the spur, and a surrounding ditch and bank, which contain the flat top of the spur, the steep sides of the spur providing good natural defences. Apparently the fort had two phases of construction (possibly similar to Kemerton Camp). An oval-shaped fort was initially constructed by digging a ditch and dumping the spoil to form a bank. Later, the fort was made rectangular and had stone-lined passageways at the entrances to the north and south. Evidence has been found for several huts within the fort with stone floors and walls of wattle and daub. There were also 42 pits within the fort such as would have been used for rituals, burials and very practically and most usually, for storage of food and goods. Local archaeologist James Dinn explains that many of these pits were lined with hurdles or basketry, while others had stone linings. Presumably much of the grain stored came from the fields worked nearby as evidenced from aerial photography as a series of terraces in the dry valley to the east.[9]

Though construction of the hill fort is thought to have begun before the beginning of the first century BC, the history here predates the Iron

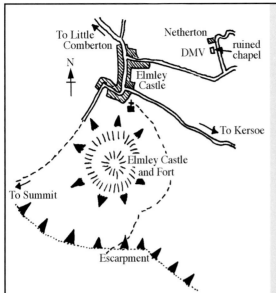

Exploring Elmley Castle

This describes the route marked to the summit on the map. Park your car in the main street of Elmley Castle. As the main street aligns with the spur of Bredon Hill, the earthworks of the castle and hill fort should be visible as horizontal lines high on the spur. Walk towards the end of the main street and turn right along the road next to the Queen Elizabeth pub.

Soon the road will take a sharp left and begin ascending the hill. Follow this to the end where it becomes a dirt track with a canopy of trees above you. Once back into the open you will emerge into a large field sloping down to the right with woodland before you. Leave the track and begin ascending to your left along a barely discernable path — this is a stiff walk — and head for the top left hand corner of the field. Notice the spur to your left and the horizontal earthworks of Elmley Castle and fort. For the summit continue through the gate up the hill, keeping to the left of any fields. Soon the path will become a hollow-way again. Keep going and where you see a farm gate ahead of you, head just to the right of it keeping the hedge to your left — from here just keep going upwards and sooner or later you'll reach the escarpment where a final push will get you virtually to the summit. The views will reward your effort. Follow the path to the right and the summit will be reached soon. This walk is very steep and takes up to two hours to the summit.

There is another path which takes you from the church to see the castle and fort on your right. This is a fairly complex route for which I recommend purchasing the Ordnance Survey map: Explorer 14 — Malvern Hills and Bredon Hill.

Age, as at Kemerton Camp. Finds from the Neolithic (4500-2300BC) have included a stone axe, and fragments of pottery have been discovered from the Bronze Age. Iron Age pottery was also found, the coarser ware probably being made locally whilst the finer probably came from the area round the Malvern Hills or slightly further west. This ware is commonly decorated with linear tool marks or rows of stamped decoration (often of ducks) just below the rim. A quantity of pots that were used for carrying and storing salt from Droitwich were also found.[10]

The site of Elmley hill fort was adopted by the Normans for their own castle building purposes, so complicating interpretation of the site, which will be considered later.

Evidence of occupation in the Saxon period (from the breakdown of Roman rule in the fifth century to the Norman Conquest in 1066) comes from the Kemerton Charter of 779AD which describes, 'the city of Baenintes Burh atop the hill Broedun', and the Pershore Survey of 972AD which describes the top as 'Urbs', or a city.[11] Most of the villages around Bredon Hill have origins in this period but this one was within the old Iron Age hill fort of Kemerton Camp. The wording of the Pershore Survey suggests at the least a large village and possibly a significant local focal point with many trade routes and paths radiating from it. The suffix

Elmley Castle seen from the air

26

Ramparts at Elmley Castle

Burh indicates that this was a fortified village which, from the overall name, probably belonged to someone called Baeninte. The absence of any fortifications more recent than the Iron Age suggests that the village essentially existed within Kemerton Camp, using the ancient defences of the fort rather than building new ones. As the centre of the fort has not been excavated, however, this cannot be proven. At a time when the Vikings were raiding up the River Avon such a hilltop site would have provided a good vantage point and some security. Nearby Pershore was attacked by Vikings in 1013AD, but the townspeople succeeded in defending their settlement, unlike their compatriots in Winchester and Oxford.[12] It is likely that Baenintes Burh was a more formidable task for the Viking raiders and that it escaped attack.

This hilltop village appears to have become deserted during or before the eleventh century because it is not recorded in the Domesday Survey. It is hard to believe that the Norman officials could have missed something once described as a 'city' so it must be assumed that the population had moved elsewhere. It could be that landslips caused the population to move as both the north and west defences of Kemerton Camp have vanished.[13] Perhaps the effects of a large population living on this fragile hill summit helped destabilise the ground in the same way that mass tourism can threaten environmentally sensitive areas. A more realistic possibility, however, is that Norman officials from the new castle at Elmley may have evicted the native Saxon population from their potentially defensible Burh/Iron Age hill fort, with its high earthen banks and ditches. The population may have moved to either the now lost village of Woollashill or the village of Nafford, substantially lower in altitude than the breezy summit of Bredon Hill.

The construction of the Norman castle at Elmley began around 1080, so as to maintain authority over the newly conquered Saxons. The castle is unusual for a Norman one because of both its isolated position and for its elevation, being between 550ft and 600ft above sea level. The founder of the castle, as well as of Worcester's long gone castle, was Urse D'Abitot, the Sheriff of Worcestershire and friend of William the Conqueror.[14] Sometime between 1130 and 1140AD the castle came into the possession of the Beauchamps, as did the castle at Worcester. The castle at Elmley became their chief seat[15] and was important strategically during the Barons' Wars (1264-8) which saw Henry III trying to resist the political demands of many of his barons. At the Battle of Evesham in 1265 Simon de Montfort, the most powerful leader of the rebels, was defeated and it has been argued that Elmley played a significant role in the fortune of the battle. Reverend Lloyd has suggested that the royalist castle of Elmley posted look-outs on top of Bredon Hill who could see the movements of the baronial forces and keep the commanders of the king's forces well informed. This led to a classic 'pincer movement' on de Montfort which proved decisive. Lloyd quotes Leland in stating that the old Lord Beauchamp sent three or four of his sons to help Henry III against the rebels and that, 'these brothers with their band did a great feat in vanquishing the host of Montfort.'[16]

The Beauchamps gained the earldom of Warwick through marriage in 1268[17] and from the fourteenth century this new acquisition became their principal seat. In 1298 and again in 1315 Elmley Castle is described as being in serious disrepair — although how 'serious' is a moot point as both Edward II and his opposing barons 'coveted' it in the wars of his turbulent reign. The castle was taken by the rebels in 1321 after using considerable force which included burning down the gates. Although the castle was no longer the principal seat of the Beauchamps, they still valued it enough to carry out remedial works and ensure it was regularly repaired after 1345.[18] For example work on the castle tower was undertaken in 1393 and on the lord's great chamber in 1411.[19] These repairs gradually declined until the beginning of the sixteenth century when they apparently ceased. It is described as still habitable in the early 1500s but by the 1540s it was in ruins and became something of a quarry for local building repairs. Leland, in about 1545, noted:

There stondithe now but one tower, and that partly broken. As I went by I saw carts carienge stone thens to amend Pershore Bridge about a ii miles of. It is set on the tope of an hill full of wood, and a townlet hard by, and under the roote of the hille is the vale of Eovesham.

It seems that after Pershore Bridge was blown-up by the retreating Royalist army during the Civil Wars of the seventeenth century, stone from Elmley Castle was once again used in its repair.[20]

At the height of its power the castle was of considerable size. The inner bailey measured 150m by 100m and was defended by deep ditches, high ramparts and a stone wall. The outer bailey was simply described as 'enormous'. There was a bath house, a nursery, servants' quarters, bakehouse, kitchen, larders, towers, walls, chapel, fishponds, dovecote, barns and the deer park which offered hunting and falconry. The lord's great chamber has already been mentioned — this was a large castle. The remains of the Norman work suggest a rectangular keep of which solely the basement of the forebuilding survives. The keep and curtain walls were excavated in the early 1900s, but no report seems to have been published.[21]

Recent archaeological work suggests that some of the castle earthworks originally belonged to an Iron Age hill fort occupied by the Dobunni who controlled this area. The presence of existing defensive earthworks perhaps helps explain why the Normans chose it as a castle site. Though the choice of such isolated and elevated sites was unusual, there is another local example in the 'citadel' on top of British Camp Iron Age fort on the Malvern Hills. The castle bailey at Elmley partly cuts across one of the Iron Age ditches which is now barely visible. The Iron Age fort was probably constructed in two phases, like the forts of Kemerton and Conderton. In this case, the outer defences are of more slight construction than the inner, suggesting an earlier date. The fort is built on an upstanding spur of the hill, thereby providing good natural defences all around. It is probable that this fort was constructed at around the same time as the others, that is, before the first century BC.[22]

The village of Elmley Castle also has a fine church which dates from the Saxon period and has some impressive Norman carvings including a spectacular font with four dragons coiled about its base. What is curious is that the village street is an extension of a line drawn from the hill fort and castle to the church. This alignment could either be coincidental or may have its origins in an ancient trackway that connected with the old fort or maybe some of the even older remains higher up on the escarpment — such as the cairn and barrow, sites 18 and 19 in the site location map on p.11. Other alignments which occur on Bredon Hill are described in the discussion on the Bambury Stone and in the Folklore section. These alignments may provide further evidence of an early sacred landscape around Bredon Hill.

With the construction of Elmley Castle and the disappearance of Baenintes Burh, other villages around the hill grew in importance, notably that of Nafford. By 1086 it had its own priest and Birlingham was a dependent hamlet. An area called Nafford still exists beneath the hill, just above the River Avon, but little has been written about how this village shrank to its present two or three houses, apart from Canon Buchanan-Dunlop's 1958 article 'The Parish of Nafford with Birlingham'.[23] The fact that Nafford was recorded in the Domesday Survey and had its own priest indicates that it existed for some considerable time before the survey was carried out. It may have coexisted with Baenintes Burh for a time as a settlement on the river, possibly serving as a port, but its location at a ford on the River Avon would have made it a focus of attention for some time. It appears that Nafford grew as the hilltop village vanished.

Buchanan-Dunlop cites evidence suggesting that Nafford grew to become a large parish containing both Birlingham and Woollashill on both sides of the river. However, it too had largely vanished by the fourteenth century, when the documentary evidence for Wollashill becomes strong and that for Nafford declines. It may be that increased flooding was responsible for the partial desertion of Nafford — a field now called 'Gullivers' in the parish of Birlingham was once the site of a manor belonging to the Golofres, the Lords of Nafford, and this field now regularly floods. The influence of Woollas Hall, founded in the thirteenth century (now a fine Jacobean Manor dating from 1611) between the ancient hilltop and Nafford, suggests that there was also a change of focus for the population. This may also have contributed to the virtual desertion of Nafford by at least the seventeenth century when Habington described it as 'desolate'.[24] (Thomas Habington was involved in the Gunpowder Plot of 1605, but received a pardon so long as he never again left Worcestershire. He spent the remaining 40 years of his life travelling the county and recording its history.)

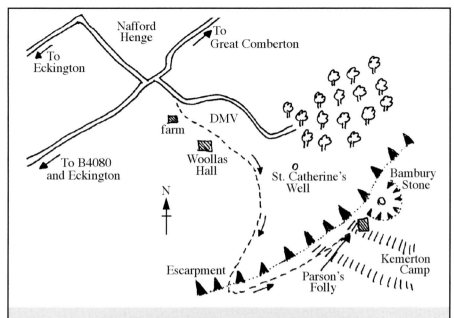

Exploring the hill from Woollas Hall

It is possible to leave your car near Woollas Hall Farm. From here walk up the track to the right which takes you close to Woollas Hall. The field to your left contains the subtle earthworks of the deserted medieval village of Woollashill. Once past Woollas Hall the ground becomes rougher. Across the field to your left there is a stream — the source of this is St. Katherine's Well. The summit can be achieved from here via an old holloway which leads up to a break in the escarpment. This is a steep walk, allow one to one and a half hours to reach the summit.

The first reference to the village of Woollashill occurs in 1275. The village is associated with the Manor of Woollas Hall, founded by Sir Richard de Muchgros. This village also had an abbreviated life and was in decay by the fifteenth century.[25] The populations of Nafford and Woollashill probably dispersed into the neighbouring villages of Great Comberton, Eckington and Birlingham. These are not the only deserted medieval villages in the area — other examples can be found at Netherton, where there is a fine ruined chapel, Strensham and Upper Westmancote, another high altitude village. The subtle earthworks in the fields give away the former position of houses, fields and roads.[26]

However, the site of St. Katherine's Chapel, reputed to have been founded by Sir Richard between 1219 and his death in 1251, is difficult to establish. The generally accepted site of the chapel (next to the well) was excavated in the 1920s and exposed foundations which could not be dated to later than the twelfth century. These overlaid earlier, possible Saxon, foundations. It could be that these earlier foundations are of a church built to serve the needs of the hilltop village of Baenintes Burh and possibly also of Nafford. However, if the later foundations pre-date the thirteenth century, they cannot be of the chapel reputed to have been founded by Richard de Muchgros. Despite this most local writers assert that this *is* his chapel. Canon Buchanan-Dunlop was the first to point out that the archaeological evidence does not fully endorse the historical viewpoint, and he developed a theory to explain these remains.[27]

In his article he set out clear evidence that both the deserted medieval village of Woollashill and the nearby village of Birlingham were once both hamlets within the large parish of Nafford which would have had its own church. His argument, therefore, is that there were two churches high on the hill — St. Katherine's Chapel (associated with Woollas Hall) and Nafford Church. In order to prove this he quoted from Habington's seventeenth century description of the area where both the chapel and the church are mentioned separately. Nafford is described as lying 'interred without monument' while there was enough still standing of St. Katherine's Chapel for him to describe the stained glass within it, and which provides the information that Richard de Muchgros founded the chapel.[28] Buchanan-Dunlop suggests that the excavation revealed the foundations of Nafford Church and that St. Katherine's Chapel remains to be discovered beneath the earth somewhere else near the well.

It is interesting that the well and chapel were dedicated to St. Katherine. This young saint was reputedly carried to the top of Mount Sinai by angels when she died and it is considered that the location of the site high on Bredon Hill is what led to it being dedicated to her.[29] It is worth pointing out, however, that the cult of St. Katherine was not brought into England until the thirteenth century by Crusaders. This leads to the possibility that Sir Richard had some connection with the Crusades — making it possible that his chapel might have been some kind of penance or chantry chapel for him.

St. Katherine's Well, as is the case with most holy wells, was probably venerated for its healing powers long before it ever received any Christian associations. Many wells are reputed to have the power to cure eye problems and skin complaints. Some holy wells have been stone lined and made very ornate and sometimes there are 'well-dressing' rituals attached to them where locals go to place flowers and other offerings. Local witches, or cunning-men and wise-women, whose services were in demand from their local populations would often use a holy well in the manner that crystal balls are now used to foretell the future of their clients.[30] Sadly, this is unlikely to be a particularly pleasant operation to undertake with the well in its current physical condition. It is probable that the cave, which was once very near to the well, was once venerated in a like manner too, as any connection with the mysterious underworld was a point of contact with the unknown.

Mention has been made of the use that was made of Elmley Castle in rebuilding Pershore Bridge after the ravages of the Civil War. During this war the area around Bredon Hill appears to have supplied a large contingent of Clubmen. These bands were formed by farmers and villagers seeking to defend their possessions from unscrupulous bands of soldiers whether they supported the king or parliament. Indeed, admission to the Clubmen was refused to any soldier. As Worcestershire was largely occupied by royalist forces during the Civil War, the activities of the Clubmen, by definition, tended to favour parliament. As the war continued and the royalist cause weakened and with it loss of control over a disintegrating army, tensions between the royalists and the Clubmen rose. On 11 November 1645, 3,000 Clubmen assembled on Bredon Hill and declared for parliament. In this they were led by local members of the gentry who, probably wisely, thought it safer to put themselves at the head of such a gathering, rather than have it storm their own properties. The force felt powerful enough to attack Prince Rupert, and also probably took part in the later siege of Madresfield Court which the royalists had fortified.[31]

The last inhabitant of the hill summit appears to have been a hermit who lived in the ruined Parsons' Folly before its repair in the Second World War. Parsons' Folly stands at the summit of Bredon Hill, and is visible from miles around.

It is suggested that the folly (being 39ft high) takes the height of the hill from 961ft to exactly 1,000ft — a claim to fame it shares with

Hull's Tower on Leith Hill in Surrey (the hill is 965ft and the tower 35ft). The Reverend R.H. Lloyd, in *Bredon Hill and its Villages* says that this folly was built around 1714 as a summer house for William Parsons of Kemerton. However, in a letter to *Country Life* in January 1960, 'W.M.' from Shropshire stated that the folly was built as a 'prospect house' for Mr Parsons of Kemerton in the *late* eighteenth century, a date that Nikolaus Pevsner agrees with.[32]

The date of this folly leads to an interesting theory which may help explain the disappearance of the Summit Cave. As was mentioned in the previous section, the cave disappeared sometime between its only recorded reference in Dr Derham's *Physico-Theology* of 1713 and Jabez Allies' *The British, Roman and Saxon Antiquities and Folklore of Worcestershire* of the 1840s which described the stones and folly on the summit but did not mention a cave.[33] As the folly was apparently built in the late eighteenth century (around 1775-1800) it is possible that its construction led to the collapse or concealment of the cave. It is sad that the creation of one of Bredon Hill's most notable features may have led to the destruction of one of its most beautiful natural landforms.

A photograph of around 1900 shows the folly in a very poor state of repair with crumbling walls, and it seems that it was only because of military needs during the Second World War that we still have Parsons' Folly. 'W.M.' (again) writing in 1960 says, 'The folly contains two rooms, but had long been ruinous when in the last war it was restored to form a signalling station.'[34] It has two floors and is currently used as a relay station for a mobile phone company.

A little known fact is that this folly was built on the site of a cairn.[35] Whether this was simply a walkers' cairn where those who reach the summit add a stone to the pile or whether it was of prehistoric origin is not known. If it was the latter then it may lend further supporting archaeological evidence for the sanctity of this beautiful hilltop to that offered by the Bambury Stone (next to the folly). Whatever the case, Parsons' Folly is certainly the most visible landmark for many miles around and lends a certain character to the top of Bredon Hill that would be sadly missed were it to fall into disrepair.

The hermit's presence would have added an interesting dimension to a Sunday walk to the summit prior to the Second World War.

Folklore & Customs

The best known piece of folklore about Bredon Hill relates to its control over the local weather. There is a rhyme which runs:

> When Bredon Hill puts on his hat
> Ye men of the vale beware of that.
> When Bredon Hill doth clear appear
> Ye men of the vale have nought to fear.[1]

I spent several years in the village of Eckington and I can vouch that this rhyme does indeed appear to be true most of the time. Other weather omens from the Bredon Hill area are, 'The ratin' of the stock-eagles [woodpeckers] means more rain' and, 'I knew as it was agoin ter rain fer my ole cat was scrattin' 'er left ear with 'er right foot.'[2]

It was considered very unlucky to shoot an owl in this locality — perhaps this had something to do with the common respect for the moon and the owl's nocturnal activities. It was also considered highly unlucky to transplant the roots of parsley from one place to another for in so doing so you 'move the devil' and he would be sure to punish you as a result. It was also thought that the wood from the elder tree must never be burned for this will surely bring bad luck. Finding a horse-shoe, however, was deemed rather lucky provided you hung it above a door with the points pointing upwards.[3]

In addition Bredon Hill is rather well blessed with its fair share of spectral residents. There are numerous good ghost stories for Bredon Hill and the surrounding area — what follows are some of the better ghost stories contained in the writings of A.C. Smith in 1932, together with a few other ghostly rumours from the area. It seems likely that Little Comberton has the unfortunate claim to fame of being the most haunted Bredon Hill village. A.C. Smith relates the tale of ghostly happenings at Oxstalls Corner (a sharp left corner on the Little Comberton to Elmley Castle road). A young man attempted to embrace a beautiful young woman he saw there, but after falling right through her he literally died of shock a few days later. A dog dragging a heavy chain is also reputed to haunt this harmless looking spot. A house in the village once known as the Thatched Tavern (now Lantern Cottage) is reputed to be haunted by a nun who snatches bedclothes off the inhabitants — Mr Smith reports that the skeletons of two men were unearthed in the garden. A haunted location near the same village is Mary Brook Bridge, a lonely spot on the road from Pershore in the dip after ascending Avonbank. Various tales of hauntings come from here, but the most dramatic is that of a headless man galloping on a white horse.[4]

The Devil has visited Little Comberton, it appears. In Roy Palmer's *The Folklore of Hereford and Worcester* the tale is described in detail. A man allegedly called upon a farmer and asked him if he had any work. The farmer asked him for help with threshing some wheat and when the man agreed, he worked so fast the poor farmer couldn't keep up. Everything he told the man to do, he did faster and better than the farmer ever could. The farmer decided to test the man and asked him to count the corns in a heap of waste from the threshing, and the 'farmhand' duly reported how many thousands of corns there were. This alerted the farmer to the fact that this was no ordinary man — this must be the Devil. As luck would have it a gypsy woman called by at his house, and the farmer told her of his predicament. She told him that the only way to get rid of the Devil was to give him a job he couldn't do, and advised cutting a curly hair from his wife's head and telling the Devil to take it to the blacksmith's and straighten it out. The farmer took the gypsy woman's advice and she was proved to be correct in her prescription, for the Devil couldn't perform the task and he never returned to the farm.[5]

As if having the Devil nearby wasn't bad enough, in neighbouring Great Comberton a woman was accused of being a witch. On the 26th September 1662 Elizabeth Ranford testified 'That she heard Joane Willis, wife of Thomas Willis of Great Comberton, say that she will take her oaths that shee, the said informant, is a witch, and bewitched to death one

Thos. Right's wife, and one Robert Price's child, both of Comberton.'[6] The testimony goes on to explain that these two women had a fight, suggestive more of ill-feeling than diabolical magical arts.

Slightly less sinister, but intriguing nonetheless is the ghost of Pensham — the setting is the farmhouse known as Pensham Fields. A.C. Smith tells us that a woman was resting in bed ill with a cold when, at around 8:30pm, she noticed a strange man sitting in the chair next to her. When he began staring right at her, she became very frightened and made a run for the door to flee the room. When she returned with others he had disappeared.

From Kersoe comes a quite horrible story that I would advise the faint-hearted not to read. It is said that in an old house in the village a man decided to end his life by severing his jugular vein, and did so in the attic. There are reputedly indelible bloodstains on the floor of this attic that hard scrubbing has been unable to shift, whilst the unfortunate individual is said to haunt the roof space with his footsteps.

Ashton-under-Hill had a white lady who swept screaming along the village street, and also the phantom of a robber-monk called Benedict.[7]

There is also a ghost who haunts St. Benedict's Pool in a field above Beckford Hall. Legends vary in detail but it is alleged that there is treasure in the pool, consisting of either gold candlesticks or silver bells from the church. This is probably the result of legends dating from the Civil War of the seventeenth century where church plate was sometimes thrown into pools for safe keeping. The pool is also reputed to be haunted by a beautiful woman — it is probable that this refers to an incidence of drowning.

The final story from the 'Smith files' related here concerns a ghost known as Black Harry who, it is thought, gained the name because he was such a bad-tempered man. He owned a farm but also rented nearby grazing land. One day, when he went to check his stock on his rented land he noticed that the neighbouring tenant had moved the boundary stones and encroached upon what rightfully was rented to him. In a rather bad-tempered manner he registered his complaint with the neighbour, news of which no doubt spread about the area. Harry then became conspicuous by his absence — people were used to seeing him ride about on his little white pony and assumed that he must be unwell. As the days passed and there was still no sign of him, they eventually organised a search of the house where they found that he had been murdered in his bed. There is no mention in the story as to whether the culprit was punished, so maybe they were all just glad to be rid of bad-tempered Harry. But after the funeral he was often seen riding around on his little white pony once again, much to the distress of the locals. A priest was called and asked to lay him to rest, but his attempts failed and Black Harry continued to ride around frightening the locals. Another priest was called who threw an unlighted candle into a nearby pond after offering a prayer. This attempt didn't work either. The priest tried again and this time allegedly succeeded in laying Black Harry to rest. Another version of the story has a slightly different ending, however, recording that the priest was unsuccessful and that *twelve* priests from the villages around the hill met at the pond where 'each held a lighted candle and each said a prayer. Eleven of the candles "went out" but the flame of the twelfth turned blue. Then the possessor of the blue-flamed candle repeated his prayer, and as all agreed that the ghost had been put to rest they departed.'[8] It seems to me that the priests would have been more successful if they'd found the culprit and ensured that justice was done for Harry, however bad-tempered he may have been while he was alive.

As for other unquiet spirits, it is probable that poor old Harry Dean (who was allegedly murdered in 'Death Quarry', as mentioned in the Introduction) roams the hill on some evenings. There are numerous local rumours about hauntings at Woollas Hall, although detailed ghost stories from this imposing Jacobean residence are hard to find. However, it does contain numerous hiding holes which were used to conceal Catholic priests during the Reformation.[9] One quite well documented ghost story comes from Bredon village. An evacuee child staying in Bredon during the Second World War was sitting alone on her bed one summer's day when an enormous black dog with glowing red eyes walked into the room. The girl remained frozen with terror as the dog walked past her and vanished before reaching the door.[10]

Tunnel legends are common throughout Britain and most cases turn out to be garbled accounts of ancient lost paths or sacred ways — not tunnels at all. Bredon Hill has a few of these legends of its own. The first is at Beckford, where there is a story that tunnels radiate out from underneath the church. At Eckington there is a similar legend of a tunnel leading from the church. A piece of evidence often cited in support of this particular tunnel is that in January 1986 a large hole appeared in the back garden of what was the Crown Inn next door to the church. However, this was probably a large well or an ice house.[11] The best local example of a tunnel legend that preserves memories of an ancient way comes from Pershore where it is reputed that a tunnel links the abbey to Bredon Hill. Not only would this tunnel be a rather long one, but if it was meant to go to the top it would also pass beneath the River Avon and the village of Great Comberton. Tunnelling beneath rivers is a notoriously hazardous business and would require sufficient depth and drainage to be achieved safely. It is possible that this legend preserves the memory of a sacred way, or 'ley' alignment because the Bambury Stone at the summit, Great Comberton Church, and Pershore Abbey all form a perfectly straight line.[12] The 'dead sunny' alignment described when discussing the Bambury Stone and the alignment referred to at Elmley Castle may provide further examples of this kind of linear feature.

Another legend from the hill concerns 'Old Mother Darky'. She is reputed to have been a witch from Overbury who used to turn children into hounds and use them to hunt over the hill. Their cry could be heard in misty weather when the hill was wreathed in cloud. After a year they would be returned to their families, but afterwards they could never leave the hill.[13] This legend combines three important pieces of information. It records the popular belief, even now, that it is not possible to leave the hill once you've lived in one of its villages, and it clearly records the existence of a witch in Overbury in some long distant time. But it also has similarities with the 'wild hunt' legend, which is common throughout the world. It usually consists of a female deity leading the angry dead on a hunt through the night on a couple of occasions a year. This one is clearly slightly different, but sufficiently similar to raise the suspicion that the original Bredon Hill wild hunt myth has become confused with the folk memory of witchcraft. It may be that this myth is related to the 'dead sunny' alignment that features the Bambury Stone.

The stones on the hill have their own folklore too. The practice of passing people through holed stones at the King and Queen Stones and the custom of going to kiss the Bambury Stone for good luck on Good Friday have been detailed earlier.

Bredon Hill once had a truly magical summit. In pre-Roman Worcestershire a visitor would have been aware of a cairn, two barrows, the Bambury Stone, a cave and a holy well. Nearby there was a henge monument, two cursus monuments, the King and Queen Stones, Bredon's Norton Stones and much, much more. They, probably more than us, would also have been aware of a bi-annual solar alignment with the equinoxes and British Camp. The information in this book only scratches the surface of the many beliefs and practices that would once have occurred around this hill summit. The wild hunt myth described above may be the clue that one day makes sense of the prehistory of this wonderful place.

The Bredon Hill Villages

The villages that encircle Bredon Hill are fascinating to explore and each has a unique and picturesque charm of its own. There is a local legend (still often met with) that says, 'once you've lived in one of the Bredon Hill villages you'll never be able to leave' — their position around the hill and great age has made them very rich in architecture and very beautiful places in which to live. I've lost count of the amount of times I've driven the circular route through the villages around the hill, or looked down upon them from the heights and I can understand why people may simply never want to leave. Their beauty has a wider context, particularly evident from the top of the hill. A walk to the summit reveals the Cotswold escarpment to the south and east with the distinctive quarried cliffs of Cleeve Hill, the highest point on the range. To the south-west the Severn estuary is visible on a clear day and May Hill in the Forest of Dean can be seen with its distinctive crest of trees. In the direction of the setting sun is the north to south ridge of the Malvern Hills with the Black Mountains of Wales beyond. To the north-west the Bromyard Downs can be seen, slightly northwards the beautiful Abberley Hills and to the north the Clent Hills which delineate the urban sprawl of Birmingham. Closer to home it is possible to see Tewkesbury Abbey, Pershore Abbey and Evesham Abbey's bell tower, which survived the Dissolution of the Monasteries in the early sixteenth century. The winding River Avon travels through each of these early monastic settlements and past the north and west sides of Bredon Hill. It is within this environment that the villages around the hill have existed for over a thousand years. This short introduction to some of the features of interest in the villages will begin at Great Comberton and work clockwise around the hill.

Great Comberton

The village was called *Cumbringctune* in the tenth century,[1] and is situated on the north-west corner of Bredon Hill on the high terraces above the Avon.

The church is dedicated to St. Michael and the Reverend Lloyd suggests that it was entirely rebuilt in the fifteenth century and remains unaltered since. Nikolaus Pevsner, however, appears mystified by the architecture but says that some parts appear early Norman, meaning late eleventh century. It is worthy of note that until 1510 all burials had to made at Pershore Abbey, this village not having its own burial rights.[2] This means there would have been a burial path, a traditional right of way preserved for funerary processions between here and Pershore. While carrying a coffin this journey would have been rather wearing, particularly when the Avon was in flood.

Across the field from the church is a beautiful thatched cottage thought to date from the fourteenth century. It is reputed to have been the rectory. Many of the other timber framed buildings in the village are thought to date from the sixteenth century but some are said to be built with the timber from older buildings.[3] The tales of witchcraft and of the devil in Great Comberton (see Folklore section) suggest a local preoccupation with perceived spiritual evil. It may be that some of the cottages in the village contain objects concealed in their walls and chimneys which were placed there to ward off evil witchcraft. Objects such as shoes, dead cats, horse skulls, 'witch-bottles' and written curses and charms were often concealed in houses to act as deterrents to the evil witch. Quite often they were placed in the houses on the recommendation of the white witch — otherwise known as the cunning-man or wise-woman. In a street called Newlands in Pershore some children's shoes and other items were found in early 1999 which were concealed behind the chimney for this reason. It is probable that objects such

A cottage in Great Comberton typical of many in the villages around Bredon Hill

as these exist in many buildings around the hill.[4] Whatever the case with regard to witchcraft, Great Comberton remains a beautiful village and a great place to begin a walk up the hill.

Little Comberton

In the thirteenth century this village was known as *Cumberton Minor*.[5] The notes compiled by H.S. Hemsley-Hall in 1988 (available in the church) provide us with some interesting facts about the church in this village. The present structure of St. Peter's is thought to date from the twelfth century at the earliest, but much of it was restored during 1885-6. Above the north door there is an interesting tympanum carved with a cross and 'eight bulgy whorls and radiating lines'[6] which is thought to date from the earliest phase of building. The precise symbolism of this is unknown but they have been described as beehives, clouds, or shells. Another mystery resides in the south wall of the church near the tower where there is a rather strangely marked stone.[7] Although the origins of this are unknown it may have something to do with the various religions which have been practised here over the centuries. Artefacts discovered in the churchyard such as a glass bottle and coins dating from the reign of the

Little Comberton
Above: Ducks in the churchyard
Below: House seen from
the churchyard

43

The cross and 'eight bulgy whorls and radiating lines' on the north door tympanum at Little Comberton

Emperor Julian have led people to suggest that this church was built on the site of a Roman temple.[8] Like Great Comberton the dead of those who held land in this village were to be buried in Pershore Abbey, by order of the Prior in 1264.[9]

The village has some wonderful timber-framed buildings, particularly evident on Manor Lane which leads from the church. There are other very old buildings throughout the village. At Nash's Farm house (thought to be a seventeenth century building) there is a very large circular dovecote made of stone which Pevsner suggests may be medieval.[10]

Bricklehampton

This little hamlet between Little Comberton and Elmley Castle was known as *Bricstelmestune* in the Domesday Book. The church, dedicated to St. Michael, has some twelfth century masonry which survived the over-enthusiasm of its Victorian restoration. Both the font, with two crosses and rosettes on it, and the south doorway are of this period.[11] The burials for this church probably went to Pershore Abbey until Edward the Confessor granted Bricklehampton to Westminster Abbey in the eleventh century which 'the Pershore monks resented keenly'. In 1147 Westminster Abbey built the church of St. Andrew in Pershore, opposite the abbey, to serve its part of the population.[12] This church, therefore, became the 'mother church' of Bricklehampton.

*Bricklehampton Church and the cottage to its south-west
mentioned by Pevsner*

Other fine buildings exist within the hamlet. Pevsner remarks upon a pleasant timber-framed cottage of around 1600 to the south-west of the church and Bricklehampton Hall is just visible through the trees from the Little Comberton to Elmley Castle road. It is a large mansion built in the Italian style for the Woodward family in 1848 and is now a nursing home.[13]

Elmley Castle

Elmley's castle is now gone but it still has a fine main street which aims directly at its site. This may be evidence of an ancient landscape as the village is older than the castle, which itself was built on an Iron Age hill fort. (See also pp.26-9.)

In the eighth century the village was called *Elm-laeh*, meaning a clearing in an elm wood. Lloyd says that the earliest reference to the

Building in the main street at Elmley Castle

village occurs in a Saxon Charter of 780 AD when King Offa of Mercia granted land in the area to the Church of Worcester. He adds that the land was probably settled and cleared by the Saxons up to 160 years previously.[14] It seems that the villagers here chose not to occupy the hill fort above them in the same manner as those who occupied Kemerton Camp at the summit (see pp.21-3).

The beautiful church at Elmley as it now stands dates from before 1100, the pleasing zig-zag of herring-bone masonry in the chancel wall being evidence of this early work. The rest of the church was built in phases up to the fifteenth century. The porch of the church, which Pevsner dates to the thirteenth century, has some very interesting little carvings of a pig and a hare set into either side which Mike Salter, in his architectural survey of the churches of Worcestershire, says are re-set Norman work. This church has a spectacular font, the pedestal of which has dragons coiled about it. This is thought to be of the late eleventh or early twelfth century but the bowl dates from the reign of Henry VIII.[15]

In 1575 Queen Elizabeth visited Elmley — best commemorated in the name of the fine old public house in the village. Lloyd suggests

Multiple sundial in the churchyard

One of a number of re-set Norman carvings in the church porch; others include geometric designs

that she made this visit as part of her policy of visiting her wealthiest subjects and expecting them to entertain her, thereby depleting her hosts' resources and reducing their power. On this occasion the host was William Savage whose family held the manor here since the Beauchamps (who wielded power from the castle, see p.28) left for Warwick. Although the castle of Elmley was by this time in ruins and served primarily as a quarry for local building projects, the Queen was entertained in the luxurious manor built by the Savages soon after they purchased the Manor of Elmley in 1544. Unfortunately this fine large mansion was demolished to make way for a housing estate in 1963.[16]

Inside the church is a memorial to members of the Savage family: on the right is Sir William Savage, who died in 1616, in the middle is his son, Sir Giles Savage who died in 1631, and on the left Lady Catherine Savage, wife of Sir Giles, holding in her arms a daughter born after his death. At their feet kneel their four sons.[17]

Opposite this memorial is one to the first Earl of Coventry. It should have been erected at Croome D'Abitot church, some eight miles away — but was refused entry! The cause lay with the disputed origins of the Earl's second wife

Two views of the memorial to the Savage family

*The inn sign commemorating
Queen Elizabeth's visit*

who, after the Earl's death, subsequently married Thomas Savage of Elmley Castle. The Latin text says that the Countess was 'of noble family and daughter of Richard Graham of Norfolk'. The Earl's son disputed this lineage, suggesting that she was in fact the 'daughter of one Richard Grimes, a mean person, by trade a turner', the niece of the Earl's housekeeper and a mere servant, marrying the Earl in his declining years.[18]

In the churchyard are two fine sundials, both dating from the sixteenth century. The original gnomons are in the church, new ones being fitted to the dials in 1971. Each gnomon works, pointing to celestial north. An allowance for 'sun dial time' has to be made, as solar time differs from clock time by an amount that varies from 16 minutes fast to 14 minutes slow over the year; additionally Elmley Castle solar time is eight minutes behind Greenwich solar time.[19]

The village is wonderful architecturally, with many fine buildings in the main street and lovely timber-framed buildings up Hill Lane. This village has classic 'picture postcard' qualities which it holds despite the loss of its castle and manor.

Netherton

This small village lies to the east of Elmley Castle and was known as *Neothertine* in 780 AD.[20] There was once a medieval village here similar to those which existed at Westmancote and Woollashill, but it has since been reduced to a few houses. Nevertheless, the old core of the village can still be traced in the subtle earthworks in the fields around Chapel Farm.[21] There is a fine ruined chapel here with a wonderful carving above the door of what Lloyd says is a Saw Fish, but Pevsner thinks is a winged dragon. The chapel was reputed to have been built as a chapel of ease for the Parish Church of St. Gregory at Cropthorne, which was the mother church of Netherton before it became a parish in its own right. It is probable that a burial path existed between Netherton and Cropthorne. The chancel dates from 1200 but Pevsner suggests that the carving of the dragon is earlier and has probably been re-used from elsewhere.[22]

The presence of a carving of a winged dragon is interesting, for other dragon carvings can be found around the hill at Elmley, Beckford and Eckington. It is thought by some people that dragons carved in churches may symbolise the pagan forces which were formerly venerated at the site. Alternatively it is sometimes said that their inclusion in churches is symbolic of Christian supremacy over pagan forces — hence the symbolism of St. George defeating the dragon. Either way it may well be indicative of a much earlier respect for the place. In Netherton this could certainly be true for once there was a cursus monument (a linear double-ditched enclosure which probably had a ritual function possibly similar to henge monuments) and a pit alignment, both probably dating from the Neolithic.

The ruins of Netherton Chapel

Ashton-under-Hill walk in the woods

This circular walk requires walking boots and is strenuous in places. At least an hour should be allowed.

The walk begins in Ashton-under-Hill at the junction of Cotton Street and the main street, so you want to park near this junction which is close to the centre of the village.

Walk along Cotton Street and look for the second right turn which you will find at the western end of the village where it meets woodland. The track ascends steeply and then levels out as it proceeds through the woodland. After a short while the woodland on the right disappears and you can enjoy views out towards the east. Continue along the track as it re-enters the woodland. You will soon come to a fork in the road where, for the purposes of this walk, you should take the left fork.

The track rolls up and down through some very picturesque woodland and then descends into an area of grassland with straight lines of deciduous trees. At this point you need to leave the track and take a diagonal route across the grassland to your left in order to stay on the right of way. This footpath is marked with arrows on the trees. The change from

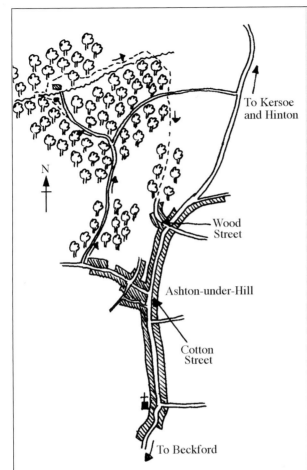

dense woodland to this open field with rows of trees makes for a very pleasant contrast.

The path across the grassland leads to a small bridge over a stream. After crossing the bridge, turn right to follow the right of way past a beautiful Cotswold stone cottage. The path curves round to the left and then enters woodland again. At this point turn right onto a path that follows the boundary of the cottage and descends quite steeply. As you approach the bottom of this slope you should begin looking for a stile in the hedge at 45° to your left. Cross this stile into a field and follow the field boundary on your right straight down to the bottom of the field. Here cross into the next field and then turn right across a footbridge. You will now keep to the right through the next two fields following the edge of the wood.

The path will cross a track and enter an orchard, when you continue straight along the path. The path will become more clearly defined as you progress along this section and then curve to the left and then to the right to enter the end of Wood Street. Follow this residential street down the hill to rejoin Ashton's main street where you will have to turn right to rejoin the start of the route at Cotton Street.

The church at Ashton-under-Hill, and the cross base and shaft in the village

Ashton-under-Hill

The village of Ashton-under-Hill was formerly known as *Aesctun*[23] and is most remarkable for its length—it has an unusually long main street which follows the base of the hill. The architecture in the village is mixed but charming along the main street, ranging from Cotswold stone with thatch to timber-framed and later Victorian red brick. Legend has it that a tunnel links the manor to the priory which existed at Beckford, two miles away.[24] Another tunnel legend occurs in Beckford. The village has expanded somewhat at its eastern end but retains its rural charm nonetheless.

The church dates from the Norman period and is unusual in that it is dedicated to St. Barbara, who is alleged to afford protection from lightning strikes; indeed Lloyd says this is the only example of this dedication in England.[25] It is therefore possible that she was chosen because of some long-forgotten event related to this site. In the churchyard there is a fine old yew tree which adds to the tranquillity of this village which nestles beneath the wooded eastern side of Bredon Hill. By the road below the church there is a fourteenth century stone cross on a three step base, with

One of Ashton's attractive cottages

a shaft and sundial.[26] There is a beautiful view towards Dumbleton Hill, which is another picturesque outlier of the Cotswolds, and on to the main Cotswold escarpment.

Grafton

This beautiful little hamlet is virtually unspoilt and long may it remain so. There was once a small chapel here very similar to the one that existed at nearby Little Washbourne. It is now a private house but is very obviously a former chapel and can be seen from the road.

Lloyd says that there is a field here called Knight's Field, so-called because Edward IV knighted some of his troops here after the Battle of Tewkesbury in 1471.[27] Another interesting point about this hamlet is the recent discovery of what may be a standing stone by Wayne Perkins (see p.12) on the westernmost track leading up to Grafton.

Beckford

The village was formerly known as *Beccanforda*.[28] Reference to the church is made in documents of 803AD[29] and it was found to have distinct Saxon foundations when it was restored in 1911. Indeed, the church

A view across the churchyard at Beckford

The tympanum on the south doorway at Beckford

54

Left: the chancel arch. Right: the centaur on the left pillar on the arch

started its life as a Saxon monastery, like that at Bredon on the western side of the hill. The church has many fine and unusual early Norman carvings which, like so many such carvings, often have little relevance to modern Christian worship. There are demonic heads and a centaur on a column on the north side of the chancel arch, whilst above the blocked-up north door on the outside of the church there is a representation of Christ thrusting a cross into a dragon's mouth.[30] This latter is clearly an attempt to symbolise the superiority of Christianity over pagan forces, perhaps indicative of the former use of the site. Of possible relevance to this is that an Iron Age village is known to have existed in a field adjacent to the present village.[31] There are many other fine old carvings in this church which can be discerned by the perceptive visitor.

In addition to the parish church which has serviced the pre-Reformation and later Protestant forms of Christianity, Beckford Hall has catered for three other variants of Christian practice. It stands on the site of a priory founded for the Augustine Canons in 1128, remains of which still survive in the cellar. When the 'alien priories' (priories existing in England but having their base in other countries) were suppressed by Henry V in 1414, the priory became Beckford Manor. Lloyd tells us that from 1551 until 1836 the Wakeman family held the Manor and allowed it to become a

Catholic centre of worship. No doubt it was also a secret hiding place for members of the Catholic community during the Reformation and Civil Wars, similar to Woollas Hall. This is evidenced by the fact that both buildings have priest holes — places in which Catholic priests could hide from secular law. Another similarity which this place has with Woollas Hall is that its current style is Jacobean, indicating that it was rebuilt in the early seventeenth century, during the reign of James I. From 1936 Beckford Hall was used as a 'house of novitiate' for young students in the Salesian Order. The building no longer serves a religious function and has been split into apartments, again similar to Woollas Hall.[32]

There are legends indicating the presence of a short tunnel leading from the Hall to the church — as mentioned the cellar of the Hall contains the remnants of the medieval priory. A legend concerning a much longer tunnel exists in the village however. Lloyd states an old tradition of a tunnel leading right through the hill to Elmley Castle, whilst a legend in Ashton-under-Hill states that a tunnel links the manor with the priory at Beckford, the remains of which exist, once again, supposedly, in the cellar.[33] Most cases of tunnel legends are untrue and tend to be a folk memory of some ancient lost path or track. However, occasionally there are elements of truth to them and this one may be an example, if Lloyd's testimony is correct. He states that the entrance to the tunnel was reputed to be found in the grounds of Beckford Hall and that an entrance to some kind of passage, 'once well hidden', *has* been discovered.[34] Unfortunately he supplies no further information and it is difficult to imagine news of this discovery being kept secret if it had been found to go through the hill, for it would be a major feat of engineering to burrow beneath the limestone cap of Bredon Hill. It therefore has to be presumed that the entrance that was discovered was in fact to some other less spectacular kind of structure.

Conderton

The most notable thing about this small but picturesque village is its proximity to the ancient Iron Age fort known as Conderton Camp. The village was settled in the Saxon period and known in 855AD as *Cantuaretun*. The village does not have its own church and has for a long time been associated with neighbouring Overbury — Lloyd says that in 1652 the manor of Overbury was known as the manor of *Overbury with Conderton* indicating

The Yew Tree pub in Conderton

the dependence of the latter. Conderton does have its own Manor now, however, dating from 1675 and the village does have a great old pub called the Yew Tree which sits on the corner of the main street and makes an ideal place to stop after a walk.[35]

Not far from Conderton and Overbury is a busy roundabout at Teddington Hands, just inside Gloucestershire, on the main Evesham to Cheltenham road (the A46). Here there is a holed standing stone known as the Tibblestone. Danny Sullivan in his informative *Old Stones of Gloucestershire* recounts the legend of a giant who lived on nearby Dixton Hill who used to amuse himself by throwing rocks at ships sailing past Tewkesbury on the River Severn. It is alleged that one day when trying to throw a rock he slipped and fell, dropping the stone which is now known as the Tibblestone and creating

A cottage in Conderton

the earthworks on Dixton Hill where he banged his head. The stone was lost for many years, its existence known only from old maps, until its accidental rediscovery in 1948 when it was re-erected where it now stands.[36] One wonders whether this was a sacred site for the inhabitants of Bredon Hill, also very close.

Overbury

Lloyd cites several names for this village in 875 AD, *Uferebroedune*, *Uferebiri* and *Vferabirig*.[37] This is a fine example of a Cotswold stone village, managed in the same old-fashioned way that it has been for years, and contains many beautiful buildings from several periods. Owned almost entirely by the Holland-Martin family who live in Overbury Court there is strict management of the properties, virtually all of which are rented. Many of the properties in Conderton are also owned by this family. Relatively little is known about the archaeology on the Overbury Estate but there have been rumours of some significant finds; there was a museum of finds from the estate within the Court but it has now gone. The Court is built on the site of the older manor which burned down in 1738 — a plan of 1716 shows the earlier building to have had an Elizabethan façade.[38] The manor was formerly owned by the Parsons family, presumably the same family who are alleged to have built

Overbury Court

Above: the nave at Overbury Church. Below: the font

Parsons' Folly at the summit. The current Court was built soon after the fire. There is a public right of way running up through Overbury Park from which can be seen a fine spring. To walk to the summit from here reveals the more gentle side of Bredon Hill.

The church at Overbury was the 'mother church' of Alstone, Teddington and Little Washbourne and as a result there may be burial paths or other rights of way related to funerary traditions associated with this church. The nave of the church is early Norman with thick columns and round arches and the chancel is a good example of thirteenth century design. There are two fine painted consecration crosses visible on either side of the chancel. An unusual feature of this pretty church is its concealed dovecote. Hidden from view from both the outside and the inside, above the chancel there is a space for 200 pigeons. It is thought that this originates from the time when the church owned the manor and as a result had the right to keep pigeons. They presumably supplemented the priest's diet. This church also has a fine font which appears to be Norman in design.[39]

One of the painted consecration crosses in the chancel at Overbury

Kemerton

The village of Kemerton was called *Cyneburgincgtun* in 840AD and once had a parish church that rivalled the others around the hill. We shall never know all the architectural details of this church as it was demolished and

Kemerton Church, largely rebuilt in the 1840s

rebuilt in 1850, with the exception of the lower two stages of the tower. This demolition was the work of the then rector, Archdeacon John Thorpe, presumably in the spirit of 'progress'. The building is reputed to have been in very poor condition but there are few excuses that can remove the sense of loss from the landscape when something like this happens. The actions of this man should be compared to many planners and councillors alive today who in the 60s and 70s sanctioned the 'development' of town centres like Tewkesbury and Worcester at the expense of Tudor courtyards and Medieval church architecture. Many other 'crimes' against heritage occur even today which

An old Kemerton advertisement

manage to go unnoticed. But at least Kemerton's original church of St. Nicholas can be seen in a photograph which hangs in the present church. It had an interesting and relatively unusual feature for a parish church — there was a small room above the porch which was used as a priest's chamber.[40] There are legends relating to a statue of an angel in the church-yard which hold that if you touch the middle finger of her outstretched hand then you will have nightmares — additionally she is thought to walk at midnight.[41] Perhaps she's an angel worth avoiding!

This village lays claim to some of the more important archaeological features on the hill, which goes some way to make up for lack of an ancient church. Kemerton Camp (see pp.21-3) and the Bambury Stone (see pp.12-5) are both within this parish, as is Bell's Castle (see p.xi). The village has much character and contains many fine buildings of Cotswold stone. One of the best features of this village is its fine public house, the Crown.

Bredon

The derivation of this name is interesting because both 'bre' and 'don' mean hill. Thus Bredon Hill literally means 'hill hill' making it, of course, quite clear from what this village took its name![42] This village sits along-side the Avon and is quite different in character to the other villages, perhaps because it is slightly further away from the hill. It has also been much added to in this century on the eastern side of the railway line which bisects it and also slightly enlarged on the western side. The core of the old village follows an approximate line from the railway bridge to the church.

Bredon Church
Above: the chancel arch
Right: the Jacobean tomb of Sir Giles
Reed in alabaster and black marble

In 772 AD the village was known as *Breodune*[43] and a monastery was founded there between 716 and 717AD. This church is reputed to have been sacked by Viking raiders around 841[44] as they came up the river from Tewkesbury, where the Avon meets the Severn. The precise whereabouts of the monastery within the village is unclear but the present church, which dates predominantly from the twelfth century, is alleged to be built near to it. The fine fourteenth century spire of Bredon's large church reaches 161ft — the only church around the hill to still have a spire.[45] The plan of the church is Norman, indicating the size of the original requirements even at this early time, and has several interesting features. In one of the recesses of the south chapel there is a slab in the shape of a shield, on which are two hands holding a heart. This is reputed to be the burial place of the heart of Sir Nicholas de Mitton who died in the Crusades and whose body was probably buried somewhere in the holy land.[46] The small size and shape of the monument compared to other Crusader graves such as those at Upton-upon-Severn and Pershore, does suggest that it is only his heart that is buried here, though Lloyd cites Mitton's will of 1290 which states that he wanted his body to be buried in Bredon and his heart at the Friars Minor of Worcester.[47] One can only assume that his will was not fulfilled, perhaps because he did indeed die in the holy land and that it was not possible to return his body as he wished — bodies tended to decompose quickly in the heat of Palestine despite the best endeavours of embalmers and often only the heart was returned home.

In addition to its fine architecture, funerary monuments and collection of fourteenth century tiles bearing many important coats of arms, this church has an intriguing mystery hidden within its walls. In 1966/7 permission was obtained to explore a section of the walls of the church where there appeared to be a hollow space. The examination revealed a room without a finished floor or ceiling. There were no signs of any stairs or any other kind of access. Suggestions for its use have therefore tended towards variations on the theme of a hermit's cell, but the lack of any kind of opening to the space appears to tend away from even this theory, as some contact with the outside world was always maintained, and at least an opening to pass food and other materials needed to exist.[48] Had the room been finished then it may have been easier to determine its intended use, but the lack of stairs makes this a truly mysterious chamber.

Adjacent to the church there are more fine buildings. The fourteenth century Tithe Barn is owned by the National Trust and is very well maintained, having been restored after a disastrous fire in 1980. This is where the produce of the villagers payable as tithes to the church was kept. Lloyd states the local folklore that the barn is one where Shakespeare performed

The old rectory near Bredon Church

Bredon's tithe barn

during his 'barn-storming' period, the same is alleged of nearby Bredon's Norton's barn. The old rectory to the north-east of the church is a large house dating from the sixteenth century and is curious because of two little figures which sit atop the roof. They are said to represent Oliver Cromwell and Charles II, and local legend states that if the two figures ever meet it will be the end of the world. It would be nice to hear an explanation that accounts for the strange beasts the figures sit upon, they are definitely not horses. Other well preserved buildings such as the seventeenth century Old Mansion and the eighteenth century Manor House make this, in the words of Nikolaus Pevsner, 'an exceptionally fine group of buildings'.[49] There is an interesting milestone in the shape of an obelisk at the entry to a lane which leads to the church. This is an extremely interesting area to visit in architectural terms.

Westmancote

The King and Queen Stones (see pp.7-11) are very easy to reach from the end of the track leading up from this lovely little village. The oldest part of the village is a group of stone buildings which can be found just before the lane begins its steep ascent of the hill, other more modern buildings appear further along the lane. There was once a medieval village with its own church, but both have now disappeared. However, some stone-lined culverts were discovered here leading towards the deserted medieval village site, perhaps suggesting the location of a manor house to the west.[50] The church was dependent on Bredon church, as was Bredon's Norton's, so it is probable that there is a burial path or other funerary route from Westmancote to Bredon church. Lloyd suggests that the name means 'cottage of the Western Man', ('cote' means cottage), a name given by invading Saxons to indicate where lived the natives (western men), who were slaves and serfs.[51] This village is very close to Bredon's Norton Stones (see pp.18-20), the King and Queen Stones and the round barrow near these (see pp.8-11). It is an ideal place to begin a walk to the summit and provides possibly the easiest ascent of the hill.

Bredon's Norton

In 780 AD this village was known as *North tun* and in 989 AD, *Nor tune* — both mean north town.[52] The only place it could really be called north of is Bredon, so it has become Bredon's 'North Town'. Its church of St. Giles is dependent on Bredon church and dates to the twelfth century. This is another Cotswold stone village and it is very beautiful. The fourteenth century barn, next to the Manor, is alleged to have played host to William Shakespeare during his 'barn-storming' period.[53]

The beautiful Manor dates from 1585 and in the first two decades of the twentieth century housed a very notable woman called Victoria Woodhull Martin, renowned for being the only woman ever to have run for President of the United States of America. She ran a newspaper in which she promoted her suffragette views, which must have taken some courage. Her surprisingly modern philosophies on free love, contraception, vegetarianism, magnetic healing, legalised prostitution and easier divorce laws won her little popular appeal in the USA and eventually resulted in her being requested to leave the country, which is why she moved to England. She subsequently married John Biddulph Martin. Although she did lecture in Britain about her beliefs she generally kept a lower profile while she was married to John and living in London. When he died around 1901 she moved to his country home, here on the slopes of Bredon Hill. It is alleged she performed seances at the Manor, an activity which had won her the interest of Cornelius Vanderbilt when she held them in the USA. Her esoteric spiritual beliefs did not in any way affect her ability to improve conditions for her fellow women — she was able to turn her political beliefs into tangible benefits. It is said that she lent out part of the Manor so that young women could learn farming techniques, and she is also said to have turned her tithe barn into a village hall. While certain of her views were and are considered by some to be rather radical it seems unfair that she should be included in books like *The World's Greatest Cranks and Crackpots*.[54] Essentially she appears to have been an open-minded woman keen on alternative medicine, animal rights and women's liberation who would have been regarded as a heroine in the 60s — unluckily for her she was born in 1838, over a hundred years and a couple of generations too early.

Eckington

Formerly my home, this pleasant village holds many interesting features. This village was known as Eccyncgtune in 972AD[55] and boasts a Saxon cross at the main crossroads in the village. The shaft of the cross has some curious indentations, possibly the result of severe weathering. In most villages the cross head was destroyed by Protestants objecting to the worship of objects (iconoclasm) soon after the creation of the Church of England in the sixteenth century. The cross head here was no exception and the current one is a nineteenth century addition. Many windows and other ornaments, paintings and relics in churches suffered a similar fate during this period.

The church dates from the Norman period, evidenced by a doorway in the west wall which has the characteristic zig-zig moulding over the rounded arch — this door was relocated from the north wall however.

Eckington's Saxon cross with modern head

Another interesting feature in this church is the beautifully sculpted Hanford memorial of 1616 — built in memory of the man who made Woollas Hall into the fine building it is today. There are some very interesting carvings on the nave roof which continue the dragon theme found in the churches of Beckford, Elmley Castle and Netherton. Although described as sea monsters in the church guide they all

Eckington church

clearly have legs and wonderful tails which taper off into fancy knotwork patterns. There are also some demonic heads with what appear to be vines or ivy leading out from their mouths along the length of the panel — similar to the 'green man' motif found in many churches, abbeys and cathedrals. It is recommended that binoculars and a torch be used to be able to properly see these figures![56]

The village boasts some fine thatched black and white houses and several of Cotswold stone and old red brick. A walk around the lanes in the village reveals the diversity of architectural styles and pleasing gardens that make this a village of some charm. The Anchor Inn, down Cotheridge Lane, is a pleasant place to stay for the night and is a good base from which to explore the area. The bridge here, like the old bridges over the Avon at Pershore and the Teme at Powick near Worcester, is a listed building of some importance. The bridge is on the main Eckington to Pershore road and most of the present structure dates from 1728-9. The stone piers, on which originally a timber structure would have rested, are, however, thought to date from the fifteenth century. It will be noticed that the stone is not from the Cotswolds, and in fact comes from a quarry at Ombersley, in north Worcestershire. The bridge appears not to have been used in the Civil War, suggesting that it was not in good repair, for other local bridges were all strategically important.[57]

When Eckington's railway cutting was being dug in 1838 the remains of a Roman Villa were discovered. This included foundations, tiles, a well and

Looking over Eckington towards Bredon Hill

many shards of pottery — it is assumed that much remains to be discovered either side of the railway.[58] The eastern end of the parish is at Nafford and here there are several crop marks visible from the air which suggest the presence of what may be a large henge monument and some enclosures of indeterminate date (see site location map p.*xiii*). The prehistoric, Roman, Saxon and Norman evidence from this parish give it a possible 5,000 year span of continuous occupation.

Postscript

Bredon Hill's archaeology, history, folklore and villages have provided me with much enjoyment and interest over the past ten years. Much remains to be discovered about this beautiful and mysterious place, but I hope this book provides at least a starting point for those wishing to delve a little deeper.

Further Walks

Bredon Hill and Parsons Folly from Overbury

From the T-junction in Overbury, with your back to the Bredon/Beckford road, and with the church on your left, walk up the road towards Bredon Hill. After about a quarter of a mile you will come to a gate to the parkland on your left, through which you turn. Keep to the footpath which follows the tarmacked track that curves gently up the hillside, following the line of the valley, and eventually you will enter and pass through woodland.

Where the woodland ends, the track meets another at right angles. Turn left here and follow the field boundary to the end of the field, where you turn right to take the track that now follows field boundaries on your right and resumes a course heading towards the far edge of the hill. This you reach having passed through a few fields *en route*. Turn left in front of the wall at the far escarpment, and the path follows this round the edges of fields, soon bringing you to the hillfort and Parsons Folly.

Keep following the wall and escarpment on your right, passing through one gateway on the edge of the hillfort, then another which will lead you into

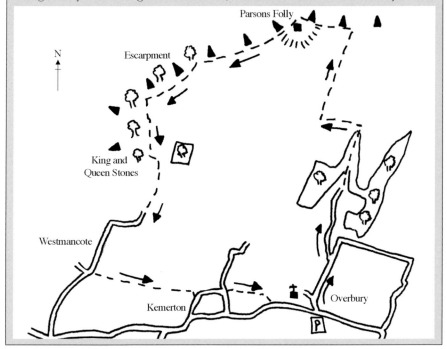

a strip of woodland. Keep shadowing the edge of the escarpment, ignoring a footpath that leads off across a stile on the left, the path you're on eventually leaving the strip of woodland through a gateway to turn left and shadow a stone wall on your left. The path drops gently downhill, passing through one field gateway and then bearing slightly left and becoming a track to more steeply descend the hillside. It passes some woodland immediately on the right, at the far end of which the King and Queen Stones can be espied not far below the path, and then makes a dog-leg turn left and then right, passing through a gateway as it does so.

The track then continues descending the hill, gaining a tarmacked surface just before it bends to the right. Continue down the lane till you reach a foot-path sign off to the left (opposite Farm Lane) at the start of a path into a field. Take this path, which follows the field boundary on your left to the edge of Kemerton ahead. Here the path jinks right and left to then pass between two houses and emerge onto a tarmacked road.

Go straight ahead on the road and follow it for about 50 yards to a T-junc-tion. Go straight across this junction and through a kissing gate into a field. Follow the hedge on your left to the far end of the field where you pass through a small gate into the next field. Here turn half right and cross the next field to its far corner, passing out through a gate onto a road. Once on the road, turn left to return to your start point.

Elmley Castle/Ashton-under-Hill

This walk starts from the church in Elmley Castle.

Walk through the churchyard on the signposted footpath which keeps to the left of the church and then leads along an 'alley', with a pond initially on your right. At the end of the 'alley' you enter a field, where you turn right and follow the field boundary around, soon turning to the left. About 100 yards before you reach the far corner of the field, you take a stile on the right to cross the field boundary. You then cross this next field to its far left-hand corner, walking towards the hill but staying just to the left of the rise in the field itself.

At this far corner, you cross a stile and descend to a lane on which you turn right. The path then goes up the hillside, and opposite a wide gateway to a field on your left, the path turns right to cross a bridge and ascend the hillside between two shoulders of the hill, and through some rough woodland. The path is fairly well trodden and waymarked, weaving its way fairly directly up the hillside, with the ramparts of Elmley Castle over to your right. In due course the path enters some woodland, shadowing the woodland's right-hand

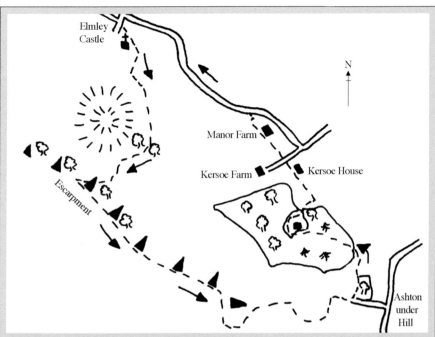

edge for a while, before slanting up through the woodland to leave it by a gate at the top.

Here you turn sharp left and follow the ridge around the hillside. You pass through a couple of field gateways, gradually dropping downhill. A few hundred yards after passing a small gate in the wall on your left and which is set in a little hollow, the path makes a sharp right turn in the corner of a field, and then after a further 20 yards, turns left though a gate to start descending the hillside.

At this point you want to follow the blue waymarking signs, not the yellow, and so turn left around the hillside onto a prominent track, (leaving the yellow route which passes through a field boundary via another gate). The blue route track will also quickly lead you to another gate, through which you pass. About 10 yards beyond this gate, you want to turn half right off the track to walk downhill, to pick up a course that shadows ancient field boundaries on both your left and right. This will lead you down to another gate, through which you pass. Almost immediately you join a track on which you turn right, and this will bring you down to a farmyard.

Keep to the lane that serves the farm, this turning first left, then right, to pass along the edge of some woodland on your left. Take the footpath signed off to the left just before you reach some houses, and follow a rolling track first through woodland, then between a couple of fields, before entering woodland again, ignoring all paths and tracks off to the right—and continuing to follow the blue waymarking signs.

In due course, the track will lead to a poplar plantation on a flat piece of ground, and here you want to follow the blue waymarked path that will lead through the plantation, then curve right round the outside boundary of house, and right again down its far side. Once you're on the far side of the house, the path then bends to the left and leaves the woodland by a stile. The blue waymarked path then leads down the hillside, shadowing a gully on the edge of the wood on your right, and crosses the field boundary ahead.

Here you leave the blue waymarked route and turn left to follow the hedge-line to pick up, in due course, a yellow waymarked one—keep a lookout for the arrows! Part way along the hedgeline you are following on your left you will come to a gateway back into the field you have recently left. Go through this, and turn right, so that you continue to follow the hedgeline, but with it now on your right. This will lead you to a well concealed footbridge in the corner of the field, which you cross, then keep to the left hand path. You will be passing to the left of the Victorian 'Kersoe House' on its hillock ahead of you, so keep to the field boundary on your left, the path soon heading into a bit of scrubby woodland and over another stile. You will then find yourself in a well preserved remnant of medieval ridge and furrow open field. Walk along the ridge straight ahead of you, with the house on your right, and out of the field at the far end onto a lane.

Here the 'fun' route lies all but straight over the lane, entering the next field by a gate, but this part of the route is quite tricky and with several stiles, so you may want to turn right on the lane, follow it down to the road, and turn left to return to Elmley Castle (turning left when you enter the village to return to the church).

If you want the 'fun' route, then go through the gate all but opposite where you emerged onto the lane, and straight across the field to a stile by a much split tree. Go across the next field to the left-hand of the two stiles, so that you are aiming to the left of the white painted 'Manor Farm'. Over this stile, follow the fence on your right to a stile and bridge to enter the garden of the farm. Cross the gardens, aiming on much the same line as you've been travelling, and just to the right of a large clump of bushes, leaving the garden by another stile. Cross the next small field to another stile, then the path follows the field boundary round a small corner of the large field in which you find yourself to leave by a stile (before you reach a field gate) and so onto a road. Turn left to return to Elmley Castle (turning left when you enter the village to return to the church).

Eckington
This walk starts from the car park on the south side of Eckington Bridge.

Cross the bridge, and take the footpath immediately reached on the right, heading diagonally across the field, diverging from the line of the river. On the far side go through a gate onto a track on which you turn right, this quickly bringing you back alongside the river. The track soon turns sharp left (the river having turned away to the right), and after a couple of hundred yards turn right at an intersection of tracks, and you soon reach a road ahead.

Turn right on the road, this soon bending to the left, and immediately after it has made another turn to the left, turn right onto another road. You will soon come to a no through road sign on the right at the entrance to Berwick Lane, and this you turn down and follow, it eventually emerging into a field. Once in the field, keep to the boundary on the right and look out for the path which soon heads off to the right to cross the Berwick Brook by a bridge, then crosses the canal and finally the Avon. Once over the third bridge, the path soon divides, and you want to take the right hand fork which slants uphill across the slope, passing through two gates to reach a road.

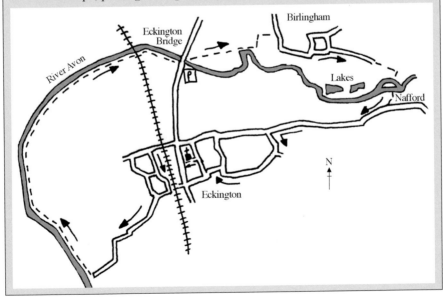

Turn right on the road and follow this in to Eckington. (For a much shorter version of the walk just keep on this road till you reach a T-junction, at which you turn right to return to the start point.)

For an interesting walk through Eckington, turn left at the first road you reach in the village (Upper End), and follow this round, it becoming Hackett Lane. Just after Hackett Lane makes a sharp bend to the right, turn left down School Lane, and then first right down Jarvis Street. Keep an eye out for the footpath on the left that leads down between two houses to enter the church-yard. Walk through this to the B road on the far side, on which you turn right to walk up to the war memorial, where you turn left onto Drakesbridge Road.

Cross the railway line, then turn first left down Boon Street. Keep on this, and in due course it will swing you to the right, and at the next bend turn left down Mill Lane, a no through road.

Keep on this and it will bend first left and then right to eventually take you down a private road to the Avon. Here turn right and keep to the riverside path which will bring you back to Eckington Bridge in due course.

The Avon south of Pershore
Take the B4084 from Pershore towards Evesham, turning right immediately you've crossed the Avon on the road to the Combertons, then right again on the no through road reached after a few hundred yards. Carry on down this road and park somewhere near the public telephone box you reach on the right-hand side.

Carry on walking down the straight road ahead of you. When you reach the T-junction at the end, turn left and carry on to its end at a high hedge. Here turn left along the farm track, leaving a barn on your left, and soon passing some glasshouses on your right. Once across a small stream, the path technically turns 45 degrees to the right to cross a field, aiming for an ivy clad group of trees and bushes; but you might find it easier to turn 90 degrees to the right and follow the track that skirts the field edge, it then bending to the left at the end of the field and following the area of scrubby woodland on your right. At the ivy clad clump of trees and bushes (however reached), the track keeps following the field edge, staying just above an area of woodland or more open grassland on your right between you and a small stream and then the Avon. About 10 yards before you approach some young conifers, there is an old gateway into the woodland on your right, a point possibly marked by a foot-path post missing any helpful signs! In any event, go through this gateway and

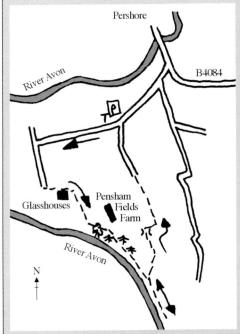

turn immediately left, to follow the path in the woodland that initially parallels the track that you were on. Soon, however, the path bears right and downhill to leave the woodland by a gate. It then traverses a small area of grassland and crosses a footbridge.

Once over the bridge, turn right down the fence line and after a few yards cross a stile into some woodland. A path, which can be a bit overgrown, now follows the river close to the bank and in due course emerges onto more grassland. The path continues to follow the Avon and after about 100 yards you'll see a footpath signpost on the bank on your left, and this is the path that you will want to take. However, it is first worth following the footpath alongside the river for a while (perhaps as far as the tarmacked lane it eventually reaches ahead), before returning and then heading up to the footpath signpost on the bank. From this post the path heads into the top left-hand corner of the field, where you cross the right hand of the two stiles into a field.

Follow the field boundary on your left to the next stile at the far end of the field, and cross into the field beyond. Again, follow the field boundary on your left (initially passing a small pond) and at the far end of the field, turn right and then almost immediately left to cross a footbridge. At this point the path appears to have been diverted slightly from the course shown on Ordnance Survey maps, and turns right to follow the bank of the stream until you reach a point where a track and conifer hedge slope down towards the stream. Here you turn left, and walk up the track, continuing straight ahead when it meets a track on the left, now walking between two hedges. (It is on this stretch that you rejoin the route as shown on Ordnance Survey maps.) At the next junction, at a crossroads of tracks, keep straight on again. In due course the track becomes a road and will lead you back to your vehicle.

Dumbleton Hill

This takes the church in Dumbleton as its starting point.

From the north side of the church, walk north along the road, soon turning left onto Dairy Lane. Follow this to its top and then carry on along the track which runs along-side the cricket pitch. About half way along the cricket pitch (and well before you reach the pavilion), cross the small stile over the fence on your right and take the path that heads at about 45 degrees to the line of the track towards the woodland up the hillside. Pass through a kissing gate at the field boundary ahead, and continue on the same line towards the woodland. Go through a kissing gate and then the path follows the edge of the woodland on your left, before it enters the woodland a bit further along and then keeps to the edge of the wood. After another short while the path leaves the wood by a farm gate and then departs from the edge of the wood to head towards Didcot Farm, reached after crossing a footbridge and then another field boundary.

As you reach the corner of the field just above the farm, turn left before you reach the stile in the fence ahead and walk up the field, roughly on the line of the telegraph poles, to the gate in the far, top, right-hand corner of the field.

Once through this gate, follow the blue waymarking signs, the path initially turning right for a few yards, then left to continue rising up the hillside, all in woodland. In due course you will find yourself shadowing the edge of a field on your left, at one point bearing left on the path (so as to come up close to the field boundary) rather than continuing on a private track that slopes downhill. Just before you reach the far corner of the field, your path turns left to enter the field through a field gate onto a track. Keep to this track which initially leads across the hill top, then starts to slope downhill near Hill Farm, on your left, soon joining the tarmacked lane that serves the farm. Follow this lane down the hillside, with its views across some of the grounds of Dumbleton Hall Hotel on your left, it eventually joining another tarmacked lane at a bend near some farm buildings. Bear left on this lane (in effect meaning you keep straight ahead) and it will lead you back to near the church.

References

Introduction

1. Valiente, Doreen, *An ABC of Witchcraft Past and Present*, 1994 paperback edition, Robert Hale, London, pp173-4; Guiley, Rosemary Ellen, *The Encyclopedia of Witches and Witchcraft*, 1989, Facts on File, New York, p228; Wilkins, Harold T., *Mysteries: Solved and Unsolved*, 1958, Odhams Press, London, pp224-230; Bord, Janet and Colin, *Atlas of Magical Britain*, 1990, Sidgwick and Jackson, London, p86.

2. Moore, Ann, *Curiosities of Worcestershire - A County Guide to the Unusual*, 1991, SB Publications, Market Drayton, Shropshire, p47.

3. 'Huge Paw Prints Lead to Puma Fears - The Beast of Bredon', *Tewkesbury Admag*, April 21st 1995; Blow, Helen, 'Big Cats Sighted in the Cotswolds', *Gloucestershire Echo*, April 24th 1995; Williams, Martin, 'Tracker Barnaby to Hound out Wild Cats', *Gloucestershire Echo*, May 29th 1995.

Geology & Geomorphology

1. Hawkins, A.B. and Murray, J.W., 'Geology and Physical Environment', in Hadfield, Charles and A.M. (eds), *The Cotswolds - A New Study*, 1973, David and Charles, Newton Abbot, pp21-30; Woolley, Dr Alan (ed), *The Illustrated Encyclopedia of the Mineral Kingdom*, 1978, The Hamlyn Publishing Group Ltd, London, pp38-39.

2. Morris, L., 'The Geomorphology of Bredon Hill', in Adlam, B.H. (ed), *Worcester and its Region - Field Studies in the Former County of Worcestershire*, The Worcester Branch of the Geographical Association, 1974, p180.

3. Mowbray, Vicky, 'An Analysis of the Geotechnical Properties of Three Rotational Slumps on Bredon Hill to Determine the Factors Responsible for Their Instability', 1998, submitted as part requirement of BSc. Hons Degree at University College Worcester.

4. Thanks must be extended to Miss Ruth Thornhill BSc. Hons, without whose understanding of the glaciations of Great Britain this section may have lacked.

5. Morris, L., *op cit*, p178.

6. Goudie, Andrew, *The Nature of the Environment*, 3rd ed, 1993, Blackwell, Oxford, p60.

7. Hails, J.R., *Applied Geomorphology*, 1977, Elsevier Scientific Publishing Company.

8. Gerrard, J. and Morris, L., *Mass Movement Forms and Processes on Bredon Hill, Worcestershire*, 1981, University of Birmingham Working Paper Series 10.

9. Morris, L., *op cit*.

10. Mowbray, *op cit*.

11. Morris, L., *op cit*, p178.

12. Curry, David, *Hertfordshire Puddingstone*, 1998, Museum of St. Albans, Hertfordshire. This is a small leaflet produced by the museum and David is not explicitly mentioned as the author.

Standing Stones & the Early Presence of Man

1. Service, Alastair and Bradbury, Jean, *The Standing Stones of Europe - A Guide to the Great Megalithic Monuments*, 1993 revised edition (1979 1st ed), Weidenfeld and Nicholson, London, p10.

2. Devereux, Paul, *Places of Power*, 1990, Blandford, London.

3. Morris, L., 'The Geomorphology of Bredon Hill', in Adlam, B.H. (ed), *Worcester and its Region - Field Studies in the Former County of Worcestershire*, The Worcester Branch of the Geographical Association, 1974, p178.

4. My most detailed analysis of this site appeared as, 'When is a rock not just a rock?', *3rd Stone*, issue 28, October-December 1997, pp27-30.

5. Lees, Edwin, 'Joint meeting with Malvern Field Club to ... the King and Queen. . .', Monday 4th August 1873, *The Transactions of the Worcestershire Naturalists' Club*, 1847-1896, p202; for the passing through ritual see Hand, Wayland D., *Magical Medicine*, 1980, University of California Press, London, chapter 11; for a brief description of Men-an-Tol see Bord, Janet and Colin, *A Guide to Ancient Sites in Britain*, 1979, Paladin, London, p21; Lloyd, Rev. R.H., *Bredon Hill and its Villages*, 8th ed 1987 (1st ed 1967), privately published, pp69-71; Mercier, Mrs Jerome, *By the King and Queen*, 1906, Simpkin Marshall and co., London, frontispiece.

6. *The Woolhope Club Transactions* 1902-3-4, 'Field Trip to Bredon Hill', Thursday 28th August 1902, p51 and Lloyd, *op cit*, p71.

7. Lees, 'Joint meeting. ..', *op cit*, p202.

8. Lloyd, *op cit*, p71; Clarke, David and Roberts, Andy, *Twilight of the Celtic Gods - An Exploration of Britain's Hidden Pagan Traditions*, 1996, Blandford, p48.

9. My thanks to Mrs Lily O'Sullivan of Westmancote for being the first to draw my attention to the use of these stones as stocks and to Duncan Brown, formerly of the County Sites and Monuments Record, for confirming this based on a photograph of the site.

10. Thomas, Nicholas, 'A Double Beaker Burial on Bredon Hill', *Transactions of the Birmingham Archaeological Society*, 1967, vol 82, OUP.

11. See note 2 above.

12. Morris L., *op cit*.

13. Watson, Bruce, 'A Watching Brief on Bredon Hill Iron Age Fort, 1985', *Transactions of the Worcestershire Archaeological Society*. 3rd series, vol 11, 1988, (pp71-75) p73.

14. Allies, Jabez, *The British, Roman, and Saxon Antiquities and Folklore of Worcestershire*, 1840s (date uncertain as frontispiece missing from copy I looked at), John Russel Smith, London, pp363-5.

15. Lloyd, *op cit*, p6; Allies, *op cit*, pp363-365; Derham, Dr, *Physico-Theology*, 1713, quoted in Allies, *op cit*, p80.

16. This alignment was described in my article 'Dead Sunny', in *The Ley Hunter*, issue 125, Autumn 1996, pp14-16.

17. Curry, Patrick, *Prophecy and Power - Astrology in Early Modern England*, 1989, Princeton University Press, New Jersey.

18. Woodward, Alfred, 'Burial Road or a Pilgrim's Way Myth or Legend', in Drinkwater, Peter, *Soliloquies of Old Shipston*, 1979, privately published, pp145-153; Bloom, J. Harvey, *Folklore, Old Customs and Superstitions in Shakespeare Land*, 1929.

19. Atkins, Meg Elizabeth, *Haunted Warwickshire*, 1981, Robert Hale, London, p51.

20. Allies, *op cit*.

21. See note 14.

22. Lloyd, *op cit*, pp67-8.

23. Wessels, Anton, *Europe: Was it Ever Really Christian?*, 1995, SCM Press, London, p160.

24. Lloyd, *op cit*, p68; Watson, *op cit*, p73; Allies, *op cit*; also see the section on Folklore for further details.

25. Willey, Basil, *The Eighteenth Century Background*, 1974, Chatto and Windus, London, pp27-57.

26. Derham, Dr, from *Physico-Theology. . .*, 1713, p70, quoted in Allies, *op cit*, p80.

27. Dinn, James, 'Conderton Camp', in Pounds, N.J.G. (ed), 'The Worcester Area', a supplement to the *Archaeological Journal*, vol 152, 1995, The Royal Archaeological Institute, p20.

28. Worcestershire Sites and Monuments Record, University College Worcester, Henwick Grove, Worcester, WR2 6AJ, no.07651.

29. This resulted in a short article entitled, 'A Worcestershire Stone Puzzle', *3rd Stone*, issue 19, Autumn/Winter 1994, p14.

30. The map contained in SMR file no.07651, derived from a field visit in the 1970s, clearly shows another group of stones in the field.

31. These stones were identified when I visited the site in January 1999 – the County Archaeological Service were promptly notified and have visited the site.

32. Thomas, *op cit*.

The Bronze Age to Recent Times

1. Thomas, Nicholas, 'A Double Beaker Burial on Bredon Hill', *Transactions of the Birmingham Archaeological Society*, 1967, vol 82, OUP.
2. Hencken, T.C., 'The Excavations of the Iron Age Camp on Bredon Hill, Gloucestershire, 1935-7', *Archaeological Journal*, 95, 1937 (1938), pp1-111.
3. Dinn, James, 'Bredon Hill Fort', in Pounds, N.J.G. (ed), 'The Worcester Area', a supplement to the *Archaeological Journal*, vol 152, 1995, The Royal Archaeological Institute, pp21-22.
4. Worcestershire Sites and Monuments Record (hereafter WSMR), University College Worcester, Henwick Grove, Worcester, WR2 6AJ, no.03943.
5. Dinn, *op cit*, pp21-22.
6. Adkins, Lesley and Roy, *The Handbook of British Archaeology*, 1998 edition (1982), Constable, London, p94.
7. Hoggard, Brian, 'British Beasts of Old', *White Dragon*, no 14, Imbolc 1997, pp18-20.
8. WSMR, *op cit*, no.03943.
9. Dinn, *op cit*, pp20-1.
10. Thomas, Nicholas, 'The Excavations at Conderton Camp, Bredon Hill, 1958-9', *The Transactions of the Cotswold Naturalists' Field Club* 1959, no 33, p100, WSMR, *op cit*, no 02907; Dinn, *ibid*, p.21.
11. Lloyd, Rev. R.H., *Bredon Hill and its Villages*, 8th ed 1987 (1st ed 1967), privately published, p64.
12. Lawson, Rev F.R., *The Abbey Church of Pershore*, 1915 (1946 edition), privately published, p33.
13. Dinn, *op cit*, pp21-22.
14. WSMR, *op cit*, no. 07263; Salter, Mike, *The Castles of Herefordshire and Worcestershire*, 1989, Folly Publications, Malvern, p63.
15. Field, R.K., 'The Beauchamp Earls of Warwick and the Castle at Elmley', *Transactions of the Worcestershire Archaeological Society*, 3rd series, vol 15, 1996, (pp135-146) p136.
16. Lloyd, *op cit*, pp22-23.
17. Hilton, R.H., 'Building Accounts of Elmley Castle, Worcestershire, 1345-6', *University of Birmingham Historical Journal*, X no 1, 1965, (pp78-87) p78.
18. Field, *op cit*, p137.
19. Hilton, *op cit*, p80.
20. Freeman, Marion, *Pershore and District - A Portrait in Old Picture Postcards*, 1991, SB Publications, Market Drayton, Shrops, p7; For Elmley's Norman castle see Renn D., *Norman Castles in Britain*, 1973, John Baker, London, p183.
21. Field, *op cit*, p137.
22. Stanford, S.C., *The Malvern Hillforts - Midsummer Hill and British Camp*, 3rd revised edition 1988, Archaeological Committee of the Malvern Hills Conservators, p5; WSMR, *op cit*, no. 07263; Thomas, Nicholas, *op cit*.

23. Buchanan-Dunlop, Canon W.R., 'The Parish of Nafford with Birlingham', *Transactions of the Worcestershire Archaeological Society*, vol XXXV, 1958, p2.

24. Buchanan-Dunlop, ibid, p2 & p4; for Woollas Hall see Pevsner, Nikolaus, *(The Buildings of England) Worcestershire*, 1968, Penguin, London, p141.

25. Dyer, Christopher, 'The Deserted Medieval Village of Woollashill, Worcestershire', *Transaction of the Worcestershire Archaeological Society*, 3rd series, vol 1, 1965-7, pp56 & 58.

26. WSMR, *op cit*, no.01289; Dyer's article contains a map of the features at Woollashill on page 57, the SMR file 01289 contains a map of the features at Netherton.

27. The 1219 date comes from Andrews, Francis B., 'Woollas Hall', *Transactions of the Birmingham Archaeological Society*, vol XLIII, 1917, p74, that for his death from WSMR, *op cit*, no. 07686; Buchanan-Dunlop, *op cit*, p4.

28. Habington, quoted in Buchanan-Dunlop, *op cit*, p3.

29. Lloyd, *op cit*, p86.

30. For more details about the activities of these 'cunning-men' and 'wise-women' see Thomas, Keith, *Religion and the Decline of Magic*, 1971, Penguin, London.

31. Atkin, M., *The Civil War in Worcestershire*, 1995, Alan Sutton, pp96-7.

32. For the link with Leith Hill see Whitelaw, Jeffrey W., *Follies*, 1990 second edition, Shire Publications, Bucks, p31; Lloyd, *op cit*, p57; 'WM', in 'Correspondence', *Country Life*, January 28th 1960; Pevsner, Nikolaus, *(The Buildings of England) Worcestershire*, 1968, Penguin Books, p98.

33. Derham, Dr, *op cit*, p80; Allies, *op cit*, pp363-5.

34. Freeman, *op cit*, p72; 'WM', *op cit*.

35. *The Woolhope Club Transactions*, *op cit*, p53.

Folklore & Customs

1. Palmer, Roy, *The Folklore of Hereford and Worcester*, 1992, Logaston Press, Herefordshire, p118.

2. Jones, Lavender M., *Customs and Folklore of Worcestershire*, 1970, Estragon, London.

3. Smith, A.C., five unpublished folders relating to Bredon Hill, 1932, St. Helen's Record Office, Worcester, BA3624.

4. Smith, *ibid*.

5. Palmer, *op cit*, pp219-221. This tale has also been set very successfully to a rhyme by Mathew George Martin of Station Road, Pershore. The poem is reprinted in full in 'How a village sent the Devil away. . .' in the *Evesham Journal*, March 21st 1996.

6. Jones, *op cit*.

7. Palmer, *op cit*, p133.

8. Smith, *op cit*.

9. Lloyd, Rev. R.H., *Bredon Hill and its Villages*, 8th ed 1987 (1st ed 1967), privately published, p85.
10. Turner, Mark, *Folklore and Mysteries of the Cotswolds*, 1993, Robert Hale, London, pp34-35.
11. Wilkes, Nils, *A History of Eckington*, 1996, privately published, p162.
12. This alignment is also mentioned in Furlong, David, *The Keys to the Temple - Pyramids, Ley Patterns and the Atlantean Heritage*, 1997, Piatkus, London. This book describes many apparent 'leys' around Bredon Hill which should be treated very cautiously. He uses simply churches in his study of this area and does not attempt to research the origins of each site to any kind of standard. A serious point worth bearing in mind is that he has clearly not recognised the equinoctial alignment described in relation to the Bambury Stone – a serious error for an alleged 'expert' on linear alignments. His theories remain simply theories.
13. This legend was collected from John Fergusson-Cuninghame, a resident of Overbury, in 1994.

The Bredon Hill Villages

1. Lloyd, Rev. R.H., *Bredon Hill and its Villages*, 8th ed 1987 (1st ed 1967), privately published, p89.
2. Lloyd, *ibid*, p90; Pevsner, Nikolaus, *(The Buildings of England) Worcestershire*, 1968, Penguin, London, p158; for burials see *The Worcestershire Village Book*, 1988, Worcestershire Federation of Women's Institutes, p75.
3. *The Worcestershire Village Book*, *ibid*, p75.
4. For deterrents against witches see Merrifield, Ralph, *The Archaeology of Ritual and Magic*, 1987, BCA; the finds are currently held at Pershore Heritage Centre. The author, Brian Hoggard, would very much like to hear from anyone who has discovered such items as he is pursuing a PhD on this topic. It does not matter what county or how long ago – please write c/o Pershore Heritage Centre, Town Hall, High Street, Pershore.
5. Lloyd, *op cit*, p91.
6. Even Pevsner uses these terms, *op cit*, p213.
7. All this information comes from the notes created by H.S. Hemsley-Hall in 1988 which are available in the church.
8. Lloyd, *op cit*, p91; Hemsley-Hall, *op cit*.
9. Lloyd, *op cit*, p91.
10. Pevsner, *op cit*, p214.
11. Pevsner, *op cit*, p100.
12. Lawson, F.R., *A Short Handbook of the Abbey Church of Pershore and the Church of St. Andrew*, 1946 edition (1915 1st ed), W. Fearnside, Pershore, p15.
13. Pevsner, *op cit*, p100-1.
14. Lloyd, *op cit*, p20.

15. Pevsner, *op cit*, p143; Salter, Mike, *The Old Parish Churches of Worcestershire*, 1989, Folly Publications, West Malvern, p36; *St. Mary's Church - Elmley Castle*, official guide, no publication date or author acknowledged.

16. Lloyd, *op cit*, p36. The grandeur and beauty of this house can be seen in a photograph in Marion Freeman, *op cit*, p73 – this house shows evidence of several alterations, the façade being 18th century.

17. *St. Mary's Church - Elmley Castle, op cit.*

18. *Ibid.*

19. *Ibid.*

20. Lloyd, *op cit*, p36.

21. Worcestershire Sites and Monuments Record, University College Worcester, Henwick Grove, Worcester, WR2 6AJ, no.01289.

22. Pevsner, *op cit*, p223; Lloyd, *op cit*, p36.

23. Lloyd, *op cit*, p39.

24. Palmer, Roy, *The Folklore of Hereford and Worcester*, 1992, Logaston Press, Herefordshire, p25.

25. Lloyd, *op cit*, p39.

26. *Worcestershire Village Book, op cit*, p16.

27. Lloyd, *op cit*, p43.

28. Lloyd, *ibid*, p46.

29. Baker, Wilson W., *Beckford Church*, 1988 revised edition, privately published.

30. Salter, Mike, *The Castles of Herefordshire and Worcestershire*, 1989, Folly Publications, Malvern, p18.

31. For more detail on this site see, Oswald, Adrian, 'Excavations at Beckford', *Transactions of the Worcestershire Archaeological Society*, 3rd series, vol 3, 1970-2, pp7-53.

32. Pevsner, *op cit*, p77; Lloyd, *op cit*, p47.

33. Palmer, *op cit*, p25.

34. Lloyd, *op cit*, p50.

35. Lloyd, *ibid*, p53; Pevsner, *op cit*, p77.

36. Sullivan, Danny, *Old Stones of Gloucestershire*, 1991, Reardon and Son, Cheltenham, p31.

37. Lloyd, *op cit*, p57.

38. Comins, John, revised and illustrated by Stirling Lee, Elizabeth, *Overbury - A Sketch History and St. Faith's - A Description*, 1993 (1969 1st ed), privately published.

39. Comins, *ibid.*

40. Lloyd, *op cit*, p61-2.

41. *Worcestershire Village Book, op cit*, p95.

42. Mills, A.D., *A Dictionary of English Place Names*, 1991, OUP, p49.

43. Lloyd, *op cit*, p73.

44. Taylor, J.F., *The Story of St. Giles' Church - Bredon*, (date not stated), privately published, p3.

45. Taylor, *ibid*, p13.
46. Taylor, *ibid*, p7.
47. Lloyd, *op cit*, p74.
48. Lloyd, *ibid*, pp74-5.
49. Lloyd, *ibid*, pp76-7; a photograph contained in Moore, Ann, *Curiosities of Worcestershire*, 1991, SB Publications, Market Drayton, Shropshire, p45, clearly shows the creatures – I think that they may be a big-cat and a bear (?), or something like that; Pevsner, *op cit*, pp97-8.
50. Photocopies of photographs of these culverts and details about the surviving earthworks for the village are on file at the Sites and Monuments Record, *op cit*.
51. Lloyd, *op cit*, p69.
52. Lloyd, *ibid*, p77.
53. Jackson, Douglas in Lloyd, *ibid*, p77.
54. Cameron, Ian, 'Vale Lady Who Loved to Shock', *Evesham Journal*, 8th June, 1995.
55. Lloyd, *op cit*, p79.
56. Howes, Roger, *The Parish Church of Holy Trinity - Eckington*, privately published, 1988.
57. Lloyd, *op cit*, p80-3.
58. Wilkes, Nils, *A History of Eckington*, privately published, 1996, p8.

Index

Bold page numbers refer to illustrations.